Book 7, Lesson 1 Test

Find a SYNONYM for each underlined word. Circle the letter of your answer.

1. Ella took care to sand the wood until no <u>asperity</u> remained.

   a color
   b smoothness
   c roughness
   d harshness

2. The military features a/an <u>hierarchy</u> with a clearly defined chain of command.

   a dictatorship
   b organization
   c reward program
   d ranking system

3. Donna collected travel brochures that <u>imbued</u> her with curiosity about distant places and people.

   a filled
   b attacked
   c teased
   d distracted

4. Alec wanted all the hikers on his expedition to know the <u>rudiments</u> of first aid.

   a rules
   b history
   c basics
   d details

5. The thief <u>undermined</u> the investigation with a flood of irrelevant tips to the hotline.

   a publicized
   b harmed
   c aided
   d distracted

Find an ANTONYM for each underlined word. Circle the letter of your answer.

6. Autumn brought the end of the drought that had been the <u>bane</u> of the gardener's summer.

    a blessing
    b hobby
    c irritation
    d highlight

7. The puppy delighted in <u>instigating</u> fights among the older dogs.

    a escaping
    b provoking
    c calming
    d watching

8. Knowing they shared a/an <u>penchant</u> for opera, Briana seated David and Michelle next to each other at the dinner party.

    a talent
    b distaste
    c attraction
    d appreciation

9. The <u>rudiments</u> of the author's new novel came from a news story about a failed bank robbery.

    a foundation
    b climax
    c characters
    d details

10. Campaign headquarters fell silent as the volunteers received the <u>doleful</u> news about the election results.

    a sad
    b happy
    c surprising
    d anticipated

Choose the BEST way to complete each sentence or answer each question. Circle the letter of your answer.

11. Something that is <u>baneful</u> is most likely to cause

    a growth.

    b anger.

    c harm.

    d luck.

12. Someone described as a <u>buffoon</u> is least likely to be considered

    a serious.

    b funny.

    c clownish.

    d foolish.

13. On what types of things do <u>extroverts</u> tend to focus their attention?

    a private things

    b silly things

    c serious things

    d public things

14. Which of the following people is most likely to have a <u>repertoire</u>?

    a a merchant

    b a mail carrier

    c a musician

    d a doctor

15. Which of the following is least likely to be considered <u>garish</u>?

    a a white shirt

    b a gold suit

    c a purple wig

    d a red dress

SAT Sneak Preview

1. Charlie's unremitting questions — Sheila so much that she was reluctant to baby-sit for him again.

   (A) tired
   (B) shocked
   (C) amused
   (D) annoyed
   (E) entertained

2. RAMBUNCTIOUS : NOISE : :

   (A) loud : excitement
   (B) restful : sleep
   (C) agitated : meditation
   (D) wild : fun
   (E) methodical : order

3. Nicole was — being the center of attention, so she tried to — her shyness by adopting an extroverted manner and wearing garish outfits.

   (A) uncomfortable . . overcome
   (B) uneasy . . enhance
   (C) happy . . emphasize
   (D) thrilled . . hide
   (E) nervous . . announce

4. DOLEFUL : FROWN : :

   (A) mischievous : sneer
   (B) cheerful : smile
   (C) cruel : grin
   (D) happy : pout
   (E) sad : laugh

5. Although his mother's — displayed no asperity, Josh's hopes of — punishment for breaking curfew were undermined by the tone of her voice.

   (A) frown . . avoiding
   (B) voice . . serious
   (C) face . . escaping
   (D) expression . . severe
   (E) note . . enduring

4

Book 7, Lesson 2 Test

Find a SYNONYM for each underlined word. Circle the letter of your answer.

1. The grant committee has to <u>adjudicate</u> the merits of hundreds of requests for funding.

   a debate
   b judge
   c weigh
   d deny

2. The principal lent his <u>countenance</u> to the students' adopt-a-pet drive.

   a car
   b time
   c support
   d office

3. Women used to <u>gird</u> their figures in corsets designed to emphasize their waists.

   a relax
   b exhibit
   c cover
   d bind

4. Katie's <u>illusory</u> smile convinced the audience that she enjoyed performing.

   a deceiving
   b bright
   c genuine
   d slight

5. Winning the Nobel Prize will make a/an <u>luminary</u> out of a humble scientist.

   a expert
   b celebrity
   c egomaniac
   d orator

Find an ANTONYM for each underlined word. Circle the letter of your answer.

6. Jacob knew that his grades this semester would <u>disgruntle</u> his father.

   a offend
   b dismay
   c please
   d deceive

7. Since he ordered the gift just days before Jeanne's birthday, Martin hoped that the delivery would be <u>expeditious</u>.

   a wise
   b slow
   c on time
   d speedy

8. It seems <u>gratuitous</u> to pour gravy on the hungry dog's food.

   a mean
   b necessary
   c indulgent
   d smart

9. The clown <u>mesmerized</u> the children by making balloon animals for them.

   a bored
   b amused
   c fascinated
   d scared

10. Reports that schools would be closed because of the storm turned out to be <u>spurious</u>.

   a rumors
   b lies
   c exaggerated
   d true

Choose the BEST way to complete each sentence or answer each question. Circle the letter of your answer.

11. If the <u>centennial</u> edition of a book has just been printed, when was the book first published?

    a   one year ago

    b   ten years ago

    c   one hundred years ago

    d   five hundred years ago

12. <u>Countenance</u> refers to which part of the body?

    a   face

    b   heart

    c   spine

    d   feet

13. Someone who is <u>implacable</u> cannot be

    a   bribed.

    b   tolerated.

    c   convinced.

    d   soothed.

14. A <u>manifesto</u> is least likely to express

    a   intentions.

    b   motives.

    c   views.

    d   fears.

15. One would be most likely to <u>gird</u> oneself when expecting

    a   a telephone call.

    b   an assault.

    c   good news.

    d   a baby.

SAT Sneak Preview

1. PRECEDENT : PRIOR : :

   (A) outcome : inspiring
   (B) ancestor : related
   (C) consequence : following
   (D) action : energized
   (E) basis : fundamental

2. Despite their desire to support the —, the theater would not countenance gratuitous — for volunteers.

   (A) charity . . admission
   (B) arts . . jobs
   (C) community . . recognition
   (D) film . . perks
   (E) industry . . screen time

3. Management decided to expedite the new benefits package in an attempt to — relations before the disgruntled staff —.

   (A) improve . . renegotiated
   (B) relax . . vacationed
   (C) formalize . . relocated
   (D) repair . . walked out
   (E) decay . . returned

4. Although Jason claimed that equilibrium between work and play was important, he usually studied — practicing baseball.

   (A) before
   (B) instead of
   (C) after
   (D) while
   (E) when not

5. ADJUDICATOR : DISPUTE : :

   (A) accountant : money
   (B) writer : correction
   (C) teacher : school
   (D) reporter : newspaper
   (E) physician : illness

Book 7, Lesson 3 Test

Find a SYNONYM for each underlined word. Circle the letter of your answer.

1. Jon's <u>discrimination</u> was evident in every detail of his home's décor.

   a   hobby

   b   prejudice

   c   wealth

   d   good taste

2. The virus' attack is <u>indiscriminate</u>, affecting all types of people.

   a   precise

   b   dangerous

   c   widespread

   d   random

3. Mr. Browning was <u>infamous</u> for his essay tests.

   a   notorious

   b   feared

   c   hated

   d   recognized

4. The <u>malign</u> message she sent removed any doubt regarding Gwen's feelings about not being invited to Emma's party.

   a   apologetic

   b   pitiful

   c   evil

   d   straightforward

5. After some minor <u>reparations</u>, a new family will be able to enjoy the old house.

   a   payments

   b   repairs

   c   decoration

   d   adjustments

Find an ANTONYM for each underlined word. Circle the letter of your answer.

6. Detailed hiring guidelines exist to prevent even accidental <u>discrimination</u>.

   a obstacles

   b competition

   c objectivity

   d separation

7. Marc took courses by mail during his <u>incarceration</u> so that the time would not have been completely wasted.

   a imprisonment

   b confinement

   c illness

   d freedom

8. If he felt that taking his little sister to the movie with his friends was a/an <u>indignity</u>, Dan never showed it.

   a honor

   b humiliation

   c offense

   d insult

9. The United States entered World War II after the <u>infamous</u> attack on Pearl Harbor.

   a unexpected

   b celebrated

   c unprovoked

   d vicious

10. The jury decided that Justin could not have been the robbery's <u>perpetrator</u>.

    a mastermind

    b victim

    c thief

    d witness

11. The museum's collection includes a <u>smattering</u> of works from Picasso's long career.

    a   handful

    b   roomful

    c   display

    d   exhibit

Choose the BEST way to complete each sentence or answer each question. Circle the letter of your answer.

12. Which of the following is least likely to be used as a basis to <u>discriminate</u>?

    a   merit

    b   race

    c   age

    d   gender

13. Which of the following is most likely to bring a person <u>infamy</u>?

    a   cruelty

    b   kindness

    c   height

    d   blandness

14. The person who <u>perpetrates</u> a crime is the one who

    a   discovers it.

    b   suffers from it.

    c   commits it.

    d   solves it.

15. One country may expect <u>reparations</u> from another after

    a   an earthquake.

    b   an invasion.

    c   a visit.

    d   a discovery.

16. A <u>smattering</u> of French is probably enough to do what in France?

    a   publish

    b   work

    c   live

    d   travel

SAT Sneak Preview

1. Despite the nutritionist's desire to curtail the students' rampant snacking on junk food, the — of the vending machines was too powerful to be overcome by the — of vegetables.

    (A) convenience . . healthfulness

    (B) lure . . crunch

    (C) sweets . . vitamins

    (D) ease . . chore

    (E) reward . . virtue

2. Abandoning her policy to let the campers settle their own —, the counselor decided to intercede when this one escalated.

    (A) bunks

    (B) belongings

    (C) accounts

    (D) disputes

    (E) transportation

3. Although Monica was clearly —, the judge showed discrimination between bad decisions and behavior patterns, and he decided to give Monica another chance rather than incarcerate her on the first offense.

    (A) sorry

    (B) innocent

    (C) guilty

    (D) defiant

    (E) mistaken

4. ESPIONAGE : SECRET : :

    (A) painting : museum

    (B) reporting : news

    (C) singing : voice

    (D) spying : security

    (E) disclosure : revelation

5. DISCRIMINATE : CONFUSE : :

    (A) clarify : baffle
    (B) judge : evaluate
    (C) combine : blend
    (D) separate : classify
    (E) list : collect

Book 7, Lesson 4 Test

Find a SYNONYM for each underlined word. Circle the letter of your answer.

1. Kevin was surprised by the mayor's <u>accolade</u>, which was something he never expected for just doing what he thought was right.

   a thanks

   b respect

   c anger

   d award

2. After last year's outbursts, security at the championship match was heightened to prevent <u>altercations</u> among the rivals' fans.

   a disputes

   b teasing

   c boasting

   d violence

3. Only a reporter as <u>assiduous</u> as Lisa could have gotten the story.

   a persistent

   b lucky

   c pretty

   d connected

4. The real estate developer <u>endowed</u> her alma mater with the funds for a new science lab.

   a manipulated

   b provided

   c threatened

   d billed

5. Maya felt that gossiping behind people's backs was a <u>perversity</u> she could not engage in.

   a hobby

   b practice

   c wrong

   d morality

Find an ANTONYM for each underlined word. Circle the letter of your answer.

6. Store employees were unprepared for the display of <u>adulation</u> from the hundreds of fans who attended the author's book signing event.

    a hatred

    b mania

    c admiration

    d disinterest

7. Ever since his fall, Robert has been <u>chary</u> when walking on icy sidewalks.

    a hesitant

    b careful

    c reckless

    d clumsy

8. Nathan's friends think he is <u>perverse</u> because he is uninterested in getting a job and moving out of his mother's house.

    a reasonable

    b lazy

    c immature

    d smart

9. Carla was <u>adamant</u> in her belief that television was for the small-minded.

    a firm

    b aggressive

    c yielding

    d humorous

10. To see it now, it is hard to believe that the warehouse district used to be a <u>decrepit</u> row of empty buildings.

    a brand-new

    b worn out

    c sagging

    d colorful

Choose the BEST way to complete each sentence or answer each question. Circle the letter of your answer.

11. How are <u>annals</u> most likely to be arranged?

    a geographically

    b yearly

    c alphabetically

    d categorically

12. Which of the following best describes <u>ephemeral</u>?

    a brief

    b eerie

    c eternal

    d flimsy

13. Which of the following is least related to a <u>pantheon</u>?

    a achievement

    b respect

    c greatness

    d infamy

14. Which of the following is most closely related to <u>tutelage</u>?

    a instruction

    b danger

    c responsibility

    d bravery

15. Through which of the following methods is Jared least likely to <u>ingratiate</u> himself with Linda?

    a giving her a gift

    b paying her a compliment

    c forgetting her name

    d talking to her friends

SAT Sneak Preview

1. Tommy took perverse pleasure in — his young cousins.

   (A) nurturing
   (B) helping
   (C) entertaining
   (D) teasing
   (E) ignoring

2. INGRATIATE : FONDNESS : :

   (A) alienate : hostility
   (B) introduce : manners
   (C) offend : delight
   (D) charm : glamour
   (E) flatter : favor

3. Though it was decrepit when they found it, the committee — the lighthouse to its original majesty.

   (A) preserved
   (B) repaired
   (C) cleaned
   (D) polished
   (E) restored

4. The clique was bound by its — political interests, and often gathered to adulate their — candidate.

   (A) opposing . . popular
   (B) varied . . charming
   (C) common . . favorite
   (D) passionate . . ideal
   (E) shallow . . scandalized

5. ADAMANT : ABSOLUTE : :

   (A) agreeable : kindly
   (B) flexible : negotiable
   (C) uninterested : bored
   (D) yielding : timid
   (E) weak : shy

Book 7, Lesson 5 Test

Find a SYNONYM for each underlined word. Circle the letter of your answer.

1. The <u>acrimonious</u> tone in the courtroom suggested that the lawsuit was about much more than just the price of a fence.

   a bitter

   b understanding

   c forgiving

   d calm

2. Hannah's <u>ambivalence</u> about the book made her put it down for weeks at a time, yet never abandon it.

   a mixed feelings

   b strong feelings

   c warm feelings

   d nostalgic feelings

3. There was a <u>cessation</u> of outdoor practice during the heat wave.

   a rescheduling

   b continuation

   c stoppage

   d relaxation

4. The <u>inexorable</u> growth of kudzu has enabled the vine to grow rampant throughout the southeastern U.S., often covering the cars, billboards, and even houses in its path.

   a beautiful

   b unwelcome

   c remarkable

   d relentless

5. Monique's <u>infatuation</u> with Thai cooking lasted only until she discovered Brazilian food.

   a obsession
   b experimentation
   c skill
   d future

Find an ANTONYM for each underlined word. Circle the letter of your answer.

6. Javin's <u>affinity</u> for soccer started when he attended his cousin's matches as a little boy.

   a attraction
   b talent
   c longing
   d repulsion

7. The dentist's cheery personality <u>engendered</u> calm in her patients.

   a destroyed
   b produced
   c exaggerated
   d repressed

8. Marina should have known that the loud music would <u>exacerbate</u> her headache.

   a worsen
   b improve
   c extend
   d mask

9. For days after running the marathon, Scott's appetite was <u>insatiable</u>.

   a strong
   b suppressed
   c increased
   d greedy

10. Airline passengers can be searched for <u>illicit</u> materials.

   a approved
   b expensive
   c dangerous
   d improper

Choose the BEST way to complete each sentence or answer each question. Circle the letter of your answer.

11. Which of the following best describes <u>ambivalent</u> feelings?

    a opposing
    b favorable
    c timid
    d hostile

12. Which of the following is least related to someone who is <u>infatuated</u> with movie memorabilia?

    a excessive
    b foolish
    c craving
    d moderate

13. Which of the following is most likely to be described as <u>poignant</u>?

    a a comedy
    b a thriller
    c a tragedy
    d a mystery

14. Which of the following best describes something that is <u>indigenous</u>?

    a primitive
    b native
    c transplant
    d beloved

15. <u>Proselytizing</u> can best be described as an attempt to do what to another person?

    a convert
    b compliment
    c subdue
    d rob

SAT Sneak Preview

1. We believed it was — for Debbie to try to proselytize on behalf of her — lifestyle in the carnivore's enclave: the B.B.Q. Pit.

   (A) foolish . . traditional
   (B) ingenious . . active
   (C) clever . . environmental
   (D) dangerous . . feminist
   (E) pointless . . vegetarian

2. Introducing — animals can be devastating to indigenous wildlife.

   (A) wild
   (B) foreign
   (C) dangerous
   (D) small
   (E) aggressive

3. ILLICIT : THEFT : :

   (A) virtuous : charity
   (B) immoral : activity
   (C) confident : admiration
   (D) dishonest : truth
   (E) noble : obligation

4. Though he was emaciated after his appendicitis, after a few weeks Neal was back to his normal —.

   (A) rest
   (B) personality
   (C) appetite
   (D) weight
   (E) activities

5. ACRIMONY : HARMONY : :

   (A) anger : apologies
   (B) yells : whispers
   (C) discord : agreement
   (D) harshness : hostility
   (E) stillness : calm

Book 7, Lesson 6 Test

Find a SYNONYM for each underlined word. Circle the letter of your answer.

1. The manager tried not to <u>berate</u> new employees for careless mistakes, as long as they kept trying to learn the process.

   a demerit

   b humiliate

   c punish

   d scold

2. Anne tried to <u>circumvent</u> her high school's foreign language requirement by showing that she had spent summers in El Salvador her entire life.

   a deceive

   b avoid

   c meet

   d fulfill

3. The idea that you could reach the East by sailing west was considered <u>heresy</u> by many in the 15th century.

   a shocking

   b likely

   c plausible

   d impossible

4. Many holidays that began in church have taken on <u>profane</u> traditions over time.

   a dignified

   b festive

   c respectful

   d worldly

5. Hourly workers are <u>recompensed</u> at a higher rate if they work more than 40 hours in a single week.

    a paid

    b charged

    c recognized

    d indulged

Find an ANTONYM for each underlined word. Circle the letter of your answer.

6. The candidates both promised to <u>ameliorate</u> congestion in rush-hour traffic if elected.

    a worsen

    b improve

    c study

    d ignore

7. Dr. Perera <u>condoned</u> dessert for her patients only on days when they had gotten ample exercise.

    a accepted

    b rejected

    c approved

    d denied

8. Melinda took handfuls of vitamins every day, hoping to prevent <u>infirmity</u> in her later years.

    a soundness

    b weakness

    c illness

    d pity

9. The preservation society built a fence around the battlefield to discourage those who might want to <u>profane</u> the site.

    a visit

    b respect

    c avoid

    d enjoy

10. Even though he doubted she would accept it, Ari wanted to offer Teresa <u>recompense</u> for taking care of his dogs while he was away.

    a   payment

    b   a bill

    c   his thanks

    d   an I.O.U.

Choose the BEST way to complete each sentence or answer each question. Circle the letter of your answer.

11. Which of the following is least likely to describe a <u>baleful</u> letter?

    a   evil

    b   favorable

    c   hateful

    d   long-winded

12. Which of the following is most likely to be described as <u>diminutive</u>?

    a   a doll

    b   a football

    c   a book

    d   a sofa

13. Which of the following is least likely to be a reaction to a <u>heretical</u> viewpoint?

    a   anger

    b   shock

    c   agreement

    d   amusement

14. Which of the following is most related to <u>servitude</u>?

    a   choice

    b   leisure

    c   labor

    d   freedom

15. Euphemisms are used to describe things that can be considered

   a offensive.

   b serious.

   c frivolous.

   d unclear.

SAT Sneak Preview

1. Everyone — so much at the Thanksgiving repast that the entire family felt infirm for hours while they —.

   (A) danced . . rested

   (B) laughed . . napped

   (C) enjoyed . . cleaned

   (D) ate . . digested

   (E) yelled . . recovered

2. It is considered profane to — at the dinner table.

   (A) belch

   (B) eat

   (C) talk

   (D) joke

   (E) work

3. EXPENDABLE : GROCERIES : :

   (A) irreplaceable : heirlooms

   (B) renewable : artifacts

   (C) precious : sundries

   (D) unimportant : treasure

   (E) ordinary : jewels

4. Many consider it more — to use a euphemism to describe something unpleasant.

   (A) colorful

   (B) timid

   (C) shifty

   (D) abstract

   (E) polite

5. COMPUNCTION : CONSCIENCE : :

   (A) flu : headache
   (B) nausea : stomach
   (C) fever : cold
   (D) guilt : anxiety
   (E) worries : nerves

Book 7, Lesson 7 Test

Find a SYNONYM for each underlined word. Circle the letter of your answer.

1. The volcano's rumbling caused a/an <u>exodus</u> from the island of Montserrat.

    a departure
    b alarm
    c gift
    d visit

2. We <u>interred</u> the time capsule behind the school for future generations to find.

    a hid
    b stored
    c buried
    d threw

3. Don's arm was <u>lacerated</u> from slipping in the gravel driveway.

    a broken
    b sprained
    c bruised
    d cut

4. Everyone present got goose bumps from Tyler's <u>rendition</u> of "Danny Boy."

    a performance
    b description
    c portrait
    d illustration

5. Andrea was afraid she would be <u>stereotyped</u> as bookish and boring just because she worked in a library.

    a celebrated
    b pigeonholed
    c disliked
    d shunned

Find an ANTONYM for each underlined word. Circle the letter of your answer.

6. Capt. Hernandez <u>castigated</u> the sailors for not being back aboard the ship by curfew.

   a ignored

   b criticized

   c punished

   d praised

7. Lance is an <u>omnivorous</u> collector of World's Fair memorabilia.

   a selective

   b hungry

   c eager

   d professional

8. A <u>resurgence</u> in fads from the past has brought fondue parties back into fashion.

   a revival

   b disappearance

   c memory

   d description

9. Donna wanted her little brother to behave in a <u>subservient</u> manner around her friends.

   a assertive

   b obedient

   c kindly

   d timid

10. We should thank Mr. Matsuno for making this weekend retreat possible through his <u>largesse</u>.

   a generosity

   b stinginess

   c connections

   d organization

Choose the BEST way to complete each sentence or answer each question. Circle the letter of your answer.

11. Which of the following is most related to <u>colloquial</u>?

    a informal
    b archaic
    c intellectual
    d proper

12. Which of the following is a reason for an <u>obituary</u>?

    a wedding
    b birth
    c death
    d promotion

13. Which of the following best describes the two kinds of things someone who is <u>omnivorous</u> will eat?

    a animal and vegetable
    b eggs and bacon
    c nuts and berries
    d fish and fowl

14. Which of the following is least related to a <u>stereotype</u>?

    a characterization
    b generalization
    c individuality
    d judgments

15. Where are you most likely to find an <u>epitaph</u>?

    a in a newspaper
    b in a graveyard
    c at a boutique
    d in a museum

SAT Sneak Preview

1. The — of the bouquet permeated the house.

   (A) beauty
   (B) color
   (C) thoughtfulness
   (D) flavor
   (E) smell

2. Even with the scholarship committee's largesse in providing me with a stipend to pay my tuition, I still — to cover my —.

   (A) work . . expenses
   (B) borrow . . debt
   (C) scrimp . . interest
   (D) volunteer . . travel
   (E) save . . meals

3. LACERATION : WOUND : :

   (A) train : travel
   (B) automobile : truck
   (C) injury : accident
   (D) cancer : disease
   (E) vegetable : spinach

4. An epitaph on a — at the site of someone's interment stands in — of the deceased.

   (A) plaque . . place
   (B) tombstone . . memory
   (C) flag . . indication
   (D) statue . . honor
   (E) card . . fear

5. COLLOQUIALISM : LANGUAGE : :

   (A) regions : nations
   (B) sundress : ball gown
   (C) jeans : clothing
   (D) tuxedo : suit
   (E) contract : agreement

Book 7, Lesson 8 Test

Find a SYNONYM for each underlined word. Circle the letter of your answer.

1. Though he tried to act gruff, Uncle Jesse found himself <u>beset</u> by adoring children the entire weekend of the family reunion.

   a feared

   b surrounded

   c avoided

   d chosen

2. Daria vowed to <u>implement</u> an organizational strategy just as soon as she found her assignment book.

   a carry out

   b give up

   c research

   d consider

3. When a publisher did not <u>materialize</u>, Sean decided to print and sell his poetry on his own.

   a appear

   b arrive

   c exist

   d agree

4. It took Albert nearly an hour to <u>muster</u> the nerve to invite Nicole to the prom.

   a overcome

   b settle

   c summon

   d quiet

5. Dylan loved to hear his mother's <u>reminiscences</u> about her childhood in Nova Scotia.

   a descriptions

   b recollections

   c nightmares

   d jokes

Find an ANTONYM for each underlined word. Circle the letter of your answer.

6. Ever since losing her job last year, Rita has been <u>beset</u> by financial worries.

   a troubled

   b distracted

   c uplifted

   d bothered

7. When vandals defaced the murals at the playground, the neighborhood was <u>galvanized</u> to form a watch group.

   a inhibited

   b motivated

   c tempted

   d afraid

8. The Amazing Aldo delighted the crowd by seeming to make coins <u>materialize</u> from their pockets.

   a vanish

   b multiply

   c fall

   d burst

9. Jack's relatives noticed that his gestures and expressions were <u>reminiscent</u> of his grandfather's, even though the two had never met.

   a echoes

   b reminders

   c imitations

   d opposite

10. Dr. Martin Luther King Jr. was a <u>visionary</u> who dreamed of racial equality.

    a optimist

    b pessimist

    c leader

    d speaker

Choose the BEST way to complete each sentence or answer each question. Circle the letter of your answer.

11. Which of the following is most likely to be considered an <u>implement</u> for writing a letter?

    a   stamp
    b   envelope
    c   pen
    d   address

12. The <u>magnitude</u> of Grant's drive to win the writing competition surprised even him. Which of the following is least related to <u>magnitude</u>?

    a   scale
    b   degree
    c   absence
    d   hugeness

13. Which of the following is most related to a <u>muster</u>?

    a   flavor
    b   single
    c   appointment
    d   gathering

14. To <u>reminisce</u> has to do with

    a   memory.
    b   vision.
    c   dreams.
    d   ego.

15. Where is the <u>vanguard</u> of a movement?

    a   on the fringe
    b   at the front
    c   in the middle
    d   trailing behind

16. Which of the following can best be described as a <u>visionary</u> goal?

   a developing cars that do not require fossil fuels
   b making your bed every day
   c earning all A's this semester
   d visiting all major-league baseball parks

SAT Sneak Preview

1. Although the buildings are adjacent, — due to construction made it necessary to take a circuitous route to get from one to the other, making us — the meeting.

   (A) detours . . late to
   (B) bridges . . early to
   (C) hazards . . absent from
   (D) confusion . . on time for
   (E) potholes . . disrupt

2. CEDE : ACQUIRE : :

   (A) steal : forfeit
   (B) seize : lose
   (C) sell : buy
   (D) get : give
   (E) annex : take

3. Although he was — about the impression his appearance would make, Russ was relieved to learn that the casting director found such things inconsequential.

   (A) confident
   (B) unconcerned
   (C) secure
   (D) worried
   (E) annoyed

4. Though —, the cost of the ticket to Brazil was not prohibitive.

   (A) inconvenient
   (B) expensive
   (C) last-minute
   (D) reasonable
   (E) cheap

5. DESULTORY : PURPOSE : :

   (A) bland : flavor
   (B) random : chance
   (C) direct : plan
   (D) wild : wolf
   (E) precise : target

Book 7, Lesson 9 Test

Find a SYNONYM for each underlined word. Circle the letter of your answer.

1. Allison thought it was silly to expect a <u>gossamer</u> apron to protect her clothing.

   a   short
   b   sheer
   c   solid
   d   satin

2. Brad did not want to be reminded of his <u>ignominious</u> behavior during the graduation ceremony.

   a   shameful
   b   comical
   c   outrageous
   d   ordinary

3. After she became a software <u>magnate</u>, Brett often contributed funds and resources to keeping her old neighborhood vibrant.

   a   agent
   b   buyer
   c   industrialist
   d   spokesperson

4. As much as he wanted the trophy, Principal Weintraub girded himself for <u>pandemonium</u> if the team won the tournament.

   a   altercations
   b   excitement
   c   cheers
   d   chaos

5. Some physiologists believe that the appendix is a/an <u>vestige</u> that was useful in digesting the less-refined food of our ancestors.

    a device

    b nuisance

    c organ

    d remnant

Find an ANTONYM for each underlined word. Circle the letter of your answer.

6. The only <u>constraint</u> on the homecoming committee's decorative vision was the budget.

    a weight

    b limit

    c control

    d freedom

7. Ms. Patel reminded the students to handle the costume's <u>gossamer</u> fabric gently.

    a delicate

    b sturdy

    c decorative

    d inexpensive

8. To commit genocide is to attempt to <u>liquidate</u> an entire group of people.

    a destroy

    b relocate

    c create

    d disperse

9. Samantha cleans her room every Saturday, because she finds the task too <u>onerous</u> if it goes for more than a week without her attention.

    a difficult

    b troublesome

    c agreeable

    d challenging

10. The baby kept a <u>tenacious</u> grip on her father's fingers as she took her first steps.

   a tight
   b loose
   c constant
   d confident

Choose the BEST way to complete each sentence or answer each question. Circle the letter of your answer.

11. What is the main purpose of a <u>cautionary</u> tale?

   a to entertain
   b to warn
   c to teach
   d to inform

12. Which of the following is most likely to be described as something one might <u>incur</u>?

   a praise
   b knowledge
   c favors
   d debt

13. What is left after a business is <u>liquidated</u>?

   a cash
   b inventory
   c nothing
   d signage

14. A <u>misnomer</u> most directly relates to which of the following?

   a name
   b date
   c place
   d event

15. Which of the following animals could be most closely associated with <u>tenacity</u>?

   a   dolphin
   b   mouse
   c   python
   d   hummingbird

SAT Sneak Preview

1. CONSTRAIN : HANDCUFFS : :

   (A) strengthen : burden
   (B) confine : jail
   (C) free : liberty
   (D) release : wings
   (E) hinder : tool

2. Elena's shawl was gossamer, and the — material — on the zephyr.

   (A) thick . . snagged
   (B) light . . floated
   (C) expensive . . glistened
   (D) warm . . hung
   (E) cool . . folded

3. The store had a "going out of business sale" to liquidate its —.

   (A) overrun
   (B) clerks
   (C) backorders
   (D) competition
   (E) stock

4. FLOTILLA : BOAT : :

   (A) book : page
   (B) salad : lettuce
   (C) army : uniform
   (D) sea : water
   (E) cloud : sky

5. Though she thought he was —, Molly admired Don's quixotic belief that the best candidate would always win.

   (A) straightforward
   (B) unrealistic
   (C) childish
   (D) solemn
   (E) endearing

Book 7, Lesson 10 Test

Find a SYNONYM for each underlined word. Circle the letter of your answer.

1. Jeremy had no problem finding former clients willing to <u>attest</u> to his skill as a landscaper.

   a condescend

   b rise

   c swear

   d compete

2. The home economics class <u>concocted</u> special cupcakes just for the Halloween dance.

   a prepared

   b ordered

   c bought

   d poured

3. Maple syrup is a/an <u>derivative</u> of the sap of the maple tree.

   a product

   b industry

   c ingredient

   d nutrient

4. Her bright smile and relaxed manner <u>differentiated</u> Jennifer from the other candidates addressing the student body at the assembly.

   a drew

   b distanced

   c distinguished

   d roused

5. The breeze from the open windows quickly <u>dissipated</u> the smoke from the oven fire.

   a concentrated

   b broke up

   c reduced

   d removed

Find an ANTONYM for each underlined word. Circle the letter of your answer.

6. It is <u>axiomatic</u> that tomorrow is another day.

a obvious
b debatable
c unfortunate
d uplifting

7. No amount of <u>disparaging</u> remarks about her team could make Mandy abandon them even though they were losing.

a complimentary
b negative
c optimistic
d disrespectful

8. The spirit committee must wade through the <u>plethora</u> of ideas about how to spend the money collected at the fundraiser.

a multitude
b shortage
c abundance
d collection

9. The dog <u>secreted</u> his treasured bones in holes all over the back yard.

a hid
b found
c displayed
d shared

10. The <u>vagaries</u> of October weather in New England can make it difficult to dress appropriately from one day to the next.

a predictability
b whims
c temperatures
d mysteries

Choose the BEST way to complete each sentence or answer each question. Circle the letter of your answer.

11. Which of the following is least related to an <u>axiom</u>?

    a truth
    b principle
    c question
    d saying

12. Which of the following is most likely to be described as a <u>concoction</u>?

    a milk
    b juice
    c water
    d a smoothie

13. To <u>dissipate</u> a sum of money is to

    a invest it wisely.
    b spend it foolishly.
    c guard it jealously.
    d save it purposefully.

14. To <u>refurbish</u> something is to make it

    a a standard.
    b like new.
    c unique.
    d functional.

15. A <u>volatile</u> substance does what quickly?

    a burns
    b freezes
    c condenses
    d evaporates

SAT Sneak Preview

1. On days when they dressed —, it was difficult to differentiate between the twins.

    (A) casually
    (B) differently
    (C) themselves
    (D) fashionably
    (E) alike

2. The editor disparaged Will's cartoons as —, saying they were derivative of Charles Schultz.

    (A) unoriginal
    (B) fantastic
    (C) stupid
    (D) promising
    (E) funny

3. ESOTERIC : COMMONPLACE : :

    (A) accessible : abundant
    (B) familiar : natural
    (C) usual : customary
    (D) mysterious : secret
    (E) obscure : obvious

4. Bob's churlish remarks made the volatile — at the budget meeting —.

    (A) audience . . relax
    (B) agenda . . pleasant
    (C) atmosphere . . worse
    (D) debate . . friendlier
    (E) vote . . brief

5. OLFACTORY : NOSE : :

    (A) visual : eye
    (B) aromatic : scent
    (C) oral : music
    (D) sensitive : feelings
    (E) tasty : flavor

Book 7, Midterm Test 1 (Lessons 1–10)

Read the passage. Choose the BEST answer for each sentence or question about an underlined word. Circle the letter of your answer.

SCIENCE FICTION OR SCIENCE FUTURE?

At the turn of the 20th century, Jules Verne was one of the most widely read novelists in the world. Born in France in 1828, he was a <u>visionary</u> writer whose fiction described so many modern inventions and occurrences years before they became reality that the <u>annals</u> of history record him as the father of science fiction.

His father was a prosperous lawyer and wanted Jules to follow in his footsteps. Jules went to Paris to study law, but he really only wanted to write. His father stopped his allowance when he learned that his son was writing more than studying. Jules spent more and more time in libraries, where it was warm, but also where he could be surrounded by books. He spent his days studying the journals of modern science.

In 1862 he met the publisher Pierre Jules Hetzel, who the next year published Jules' *Five Weeks in a Balloon*. It was a bestseller and it made its author very rich. He made an agreement with his publisher to write two books per year for the rest of his life for the salary of $4,000 annually. He more than held up his end of the bargain, and over the next forty years his <u>repertoire</u> grew to include such classics as *From the Earth to the Moon*, *A Journey to the Center of the Earth*, *Around the World in Eighty Days*, and *20,000 Leagues Under the Sea*. With careful research into scientific advances of his day, he predicted submarines, automobiles, airships, space travel, and supersonic flight. He crafted adventures around these then-fanciful inventions, and developed characters to operate them in stories that never feel <u>illusory</u>.

The genius of Jules Verne was his <u>penchant</u> for basing fantasy in fact, so that it seemed absolutely plausible. He <u>engendered</u> wonder and <u>imbued</u> ambitions in future scientists, inventors, explorers, and builders. Under his <u>tutelage</u>, the future creators of the modern world learned by being entertained. He received <u>accolades</u> from the highest offices. Verne's works were crowned by the French Academy, which appreciated both their narrative charm and their scientific and educational value. He had the distinction of being the last man to be decorated with the Legion of Honor under the Empire of Napoleon III. Pope Leo XIII blessed his books.

When the first electric-powered submarine was built in 1886, it was named *Nautilus* after the vessel in his *Twenty Thousand Leagues Under the Sea*. The first nuclear-powered submarine, launched in 1955, was also named *Nautilus*. He envisioned space travel made possible by a giant cannon that could shoot travelers into orbit, even though it would be decades before scientists believed that humans could survive the force of such a blast.

But his creativity was more than just science. When he was a boy, he tried to run away on a ship bound for the West Indies as a cabin boy, but his father found him and brought him home. Travel to exotic places was a theme in many of his stories, and he took his readers around the earth, inside the earth, and away from the earth.

Although he spent most of his life in awe of the possibilities of science, toward the end of his life Jules realized modern technology could be dangerous if people used it unwisely. In 1889 he wrote *The Diary of an American Journalist in the Year 2890*. It is a <u>cautionary</u> tale about New York in the future when the press is powerful.

Over his career, Verne completed a <u>plethora</u> of publications, including some 65 novels, twenty short stories and essays, thirty plays, some geographical works, and opera librettos as well. At the time of his death in 1905, he was about a dozen books ahead of his contract. He was a <u>luminary</u> not only among his fellow writers, but also to those who would make his fantasies into realities.

1. As used in paragraph three, <u>repertoire</u> most closely means

   a   range.
   b   collection.
   c   duration.
   d   variety.

2. Like Jules Verne, a person whose work is <u>visionary</u> is

   a   intelligent.
   b   futuristic.
   c   historical.
   d   amusing.

3. As used in paragraph three, which of the following is a synonym for <u>illusory</u>?

    a   astonishing

    b   confusing

    c   unreal

    d   authentic

4. Which of the following are most likely to be described as <u>annals</u>?

    a   yearbooks

    b   records

    c   library

    d   registers

5. A <u>plethora</u>, as used in paragraph eight, is most likely to refer to

    a   a few.

    b   a group of ten.

    c   one.

    d   dozens.

6. A <u>cautionary</u> tale is most likely a/an

    a   warning.

    b   instruction.

    c   opinion.

    d   condemnation.

7. Which is most likely to be considered an <u>accolade</u>?

    a   reward

    b   comment

    c   publicity

    d   award

8. <u>Engendered</u> most closely means

    a   developed.

    b   imagined.

    c   produced.

    d   determined.

9. Who is most likely to provide <u>tutelage</u>, as used in the fourth paragraph?

   a librarian
   b editor
   c newscaster
   d teacher

10. As used in paragraph four, <u>penchant</u> means

   a attraction.
   b incentive.
   c need.
   d tendency.

SAT Sneak Preview

1. As used in the fourth paragraph, <u>imbued</u> most closely means

   (A) inspired
   (B) introduced
   (C) overwhelmed
   (D) satisfied
   (E) influenced

2. As used in paragraph eight, a synonym for <u>luminary</u> is

   (A) celebrity
   (B) instructor
   (C) success
   (D) manager
   (E) inspiration

3. As used in paragraph eight, a synonym for <u>plethora</u> is

   (A) lot
   (B) abundance
   (C) variety
   (D) collection
   (E) rarity

4. Which of the following is most related to <u>visionary</u>, as used in the selection?

    (A) dream
    (B) thinker
    (C) creation
    (D) planner
    (E) future

5. As used in paragraph four, <u>tutelage</u> most closely means

    (A) example
    (B) guidance
    (C) instruction
    (D) regulation
    (E) patronage

Book 7, Midterm Test 2 (Lessons 1–10)

Read the passage. Choose the BEST answer for each sentence or question about an underlined word. Circle the letter of your answer.

SPIDERS: SPIN CONTROL

There are some 40,000 species of spiders—the eight-legged arthropods of the order Araneae, class Arachnida. They are named for the Greek myth of the maiden Arachne who challenged the goddess Athena to a spinning contest. The goddess turned her into a spider for her arrogance, dooming her to an eternity spinning. Spiders are not insects, and they are only distantly related to the six-legged creatures. Their closer relatives include scorpions, mites, and even king crabs. Their fossilized remains have been found dating from the Devonian period, 400 million years ago. Most live about a year, but the tarantula can live up to 30 years.

Fear of spiders is as common a phobia as fear of heights, public speaking, and flying. The spider is a <u>maligned</u> creature, but most of its bad reputation is undeserved. They serve the extremely useful function of nature's insect control. They consume up to half of all the remains of dead insects. Without them we would be overrun by bugs, which would be busily consuming our plant foods.

Aside from their skill as pest controllers, spiders deserve our admiration for their hardiness and industriousness. They live in every climate on the planet, from temperate zones to the most <u>onerous</u> conditions: from polar ice to the hottest jungle, and even underwater. The Eurasian water spider carries bubbles of air down to its home under the water's surface.

The spider is also one of only a few animals <u>endowed</u> with the remarkable ability to make silk, and the only one to do it for so many purposes. It <u>secretes</u> the strong, elastic substance through fingerlike spinning organs called spinnerets. The most obvious use for the silk is for weaving its <u>gossamer</u> web. Some silk is sticky, used for catching prey, and some is not, used for making egg sacs. The silk is also used to create a sort of bungee cord that protects them from falls, and to create the illusion of largeness as protection from predators, as they sit in the middle of their webs. Orb weavers, the spiders that build the typical circular web, are <u>assiduous</u> spinners. They build their web every day, then tear it down and consume it to recycle it. They are ready to prepare another one in about an hour, and they spin the new one in about an hour.

Mating is a dicey business for spiders. Males tend to be about 20 percent smaller than females; the females are not particularly sentimental, and they do not hesitate to eat a fellow spider, particularly if it is smaller. In fairness, though, females often die from the effort of laying their hundreds of eggs and wrapping them in the silken sac. Eating is also a challenge for spiders. They use digestive enzymes to liquidate the soft tissue of their prey since their tiny mouths are not adequate for chewing, and then they suck the juices of the creature. In general, they are carnivores and eat mainly insects, though some even eat small snakes, birds, and mammals. A few, like the daddy longlegs, are omnivorous, and eat decaying plant material as well.

People's rancor for spiders comes from the arachnid's reputation as a poisonous monster. The stereotype is unfair, and even the dreaded tarantula lacks the poison to kill a healthy adult. Though all are venomous, very few can cause infirmity in humans. Still, it is wise to be chary when approaching one, in case you have found a black widow or a brown recluse.

1. An antonym for maligned, as used in the second paragraph, is

   a   criticized.
   b   honored.
   c   abused.
   d   peculiar.

2. As used in paragraph three, onerous refers to

   a   varied.
   b   heavy.
   c   mild.
   d   oppressive.

3. As used in the fourth paragraph, endowed most closely means

   a   gifted.
   b   generous.
   c   cursed.
   d   talented.

4. Which of the following is most likely to be considered <u>gossamer</u>, as used in paragraph four?

   a denim
   b sandpaper
   c wood
   d gauze

5. As used in the fourth paragraph, which of the following is a synonym for <u>secrete</u>?

   a ooze
   b squirt
   c produce
   d spit

6. Someone who is <u>chary</u> would be considered

   a cautious.
   b intelligent.
   c quick.
   d sly.

7. As used in paragraph six, <u>rancor</u> most closely means

   a disgust.
   b hatred.
   c fascination.
   d fear.

8. As used in paragraph five, <u>liquidate</u> means

   a freeze.
   b evaporate.
   c shrink.
   d destroy.

9. As used in the fourth paragraph, all of the following are synonyms for <u>assiduous</u> except

   a diligent.
   b tireless.
   c persistent.
   d talented.

10. Which of the following are usually considered <u>omnivorous</u>, as used in the fifth paragraph?

a humans

b rabbits

c sharks

d vegetarians

SAT Sneak Preview

1. As used in the sixth paragraph, <u>stereotype</u> most closely means

(A) group

(B) standard

(C) category

(D) organization

(E) generalization

2. Which of the following is most likely to be considered an <u>infirmity</u>?

(A) paralysis

(B) fear

(C) strength

(D) hunger

(E) intelligence

3. Which of the following is most likely to be called <u>assiduous</u>?

(A) house pet

(B) infant

(C) workaholic

(D) vacationer

(E) retiree

4. As used in paragraph six, an antonym for <u>chary</u> is

(A) guarded

(B) hesitant

(C) cautious

(D) careful

(E) impatient

5. A synonym for <u>maligned</u> is

   (A) studied
   (B) slandered
   (C) difficult
   (D) feared
   (E) encountered

Book 7, Lesson 11 Test

Find a SYNONYM for each underlined word. Circle the letter of your answer.

1. It took Mississippi's Gulf Coast years to recover from the <u>cataclysm</u> of Hurricane Camille.

   a destruction
   b catastrophe
   c floods
   d terror

2. Brooke loves it when her father takes her out for <u>gourmet</u> meals on special occasions.

   a high-quality
   b home style
   c junk food
   d picnic

3. Jonah thought speaking in a <u>grandiloquent</u> style made him sound smarter, but it actually just annoyed his listeners.

   a scientific
   b literary
   c pompous
   d verbose

4. Seed companies jealously guard the genetic secrets of the <u>hybrid</u> plants they produce.

   a cousin
   b crossbreed
   c likeness
   d species

5. Hucksters used to sell snake oil as a <u>panacea</u> in traveling medicine shows.

   a cure-all
   b antibiotic
   c hair tonic
   d therapy

Find an ANTONYM for each underlined word. Circle the letter of your answer.

6. The city that <u>burgeoned</u> during the tech boom has now returned to a quieter pace of life.

   a flourished

   b expanded

   c deteriorated

   d lingered

7. Matt enjoyed the <u>grandiloquence</u> of Hamlet's soliloquy.

   a plainness

   b loftiness

   c determination

   d desperation

8. Kristin performed <u>manifold</u> duties as the store manager.

   a unique

   b various

   c difficult

   d risky

9. Though she had the support of the area's elite, what the councilor really wanted was the trust of the city's <u>plebeian</u> families.

   a exclusive

   b backward

   c common

   d refined

10. The <u>scourge</u> of domestic violence affects all kinds of families.

   a evil

   b benefit

   c creation

   d rarity

Choose the BEST way to complete each sentence or answer each question. Circle the letter of your answer.

11. Which of the following is least likely to be described as <u>cataclysmic</u>?

    a an earthquake

    b a flood

    c a volcano

    d frost

12. A person described as a <u>gourmet</u> is interested in what?

    a food

    b clothing

    c movies

    d travel

13. When is a negotiation likely to end in <u>stalemate</u>?

    a when neither side cares very much

    b when one side cares much more than the other

    c when both sides are equally strong

    d when one side gives in

14. Which of the following climates is most likely to be described as <u>temperate</u>?

    a desert

    b tundra

    c jungle

    d pastureland

15. Something that is <u>palatable</u> is most closely related to what sense?

    a taste

    b touch

    c smell

    d sight

SAT Sneak Preview

1. Tex-Mex is a regional hybrid cuisine, and though often denigrated as —, its popularity is —

    (A) fancy . . slipping
    (B) fattening . . stagnant
    (C) derivative . . enormous
    (D) delicious . . growing
    (E) fantastic . . blooming

2. AGRARIAN : CROPS : :

    (A) automotive : cars
    (B) monetary : reserves
    (C) vegetarian : seeds
    (D) slippery : water
    (E) sectarian : state

3. Though it is considered a —, many people do not find caviar at all palatable.

    (A) snack
    (B) necessity
    (C) luxury
    (D) rarity
    (E) delicacy

4. Although they expected to be scourged if caught, the vandals — their assaults on neighborhood street signs.

    (A) stopped
    (B) delayed
    (C) interrupted
    (D) continued
    (E) admitted

5. CULINARY : FOOD : :

    (A) military : strategy
    (B) literary : books
    (C) dietary : calories
    (D) extraordinary : rarity
    (E) dairy : cheese

Book 7, Lesson 12 Test

Find a SYNONYM for each underlined word. Circle the letter of your answer.

1. Frances found <u>catharsis</u> after her attack by attending kickboxing classes every other day.

   a   relief

   b   strength

   c   unrest

   d   upheaval

2. The district attorney set out to prove that the street vendor was actually a <u>cohort</u> of the convicted drug dealer.

   a   acquaintance

   b   relative

   c   friend

   d   accomplice

3. Iago made <u>diabolical</u> plans to ruin Othello's life.

   a   complicated

   b   outrageous

   c   evil

   d   laughable

4. Hecklers who <u>gibed</u> the sharp-tongued comedian soon wished they hadn't.

   a   taunted

   b   insulted

   c   distracted

   d   interrupted

5. Our global <u>odyssey</u> included stops on six continents.

   a   visits

   b   ordeal

   c   vacation

   d   journey

Find an ANTONYM for each underlined word. Circle the letter of your answer.

6. "Waste not; want not" is the <u>aphorism</u> of the conservationist.

   a   motto
   b   adage
   c   fallacy
   d   saying

7. The bartender was found to be <u>culpable</u> in the crash, since he had served alcohol to the driver.

   a   blameless
   b   responsible
   c   guilty
   d   innocent

8. The water-rationing law <u>necessitates</u> a strict lawn-watering schedule.

   a   demands
   b   requests
   c   requires
   d   describes

9. The entire senior class became <u>partisans</u> for the cause of voter registration.

   a   advocates
   b   obstacles
   c   proselytizers
   d   witnesses

10. <u>Scurrilous</u> stories about Catherine the Great are still repeated centuries after her death.

   a   insulting
   b   complimentary
   c   exaggerated
   d   fantastic

Choose the BEST way to complete each sentence or answer each question. Circle the letter of your answer.

11. A <u>cathartic</u> experience is least likely to be described as

    a cleansing.

    b renewing.

    c burdensome.

    d demanding.

12. <u>Culpability</u> is least related to which of the following?

    a blame

    b innocence

    c fault

    d responsibility

13. What is a band of <u>partisans</u> most likely to oppose?

    a an uprising

    b a rebellion

    c an occupation

    d a free election

14. <u>Posterity</u> most refers to a person's

    a ancestors.

    b peers.

    c descendants.

    d enemies.

15. An <u>enormity</u> is least likely to be which of the following?

    a small

    b boring

    c enormous

    d immoderate

SAT Sneak Preview

1. COHORT : TEAM : :

   (A) battalion : individual
   (B) class : grade
   (C) aide : assistant
   (D) group : line
   (E) associate : system

2. Since Jeanne considered her gibe about his shoes innocuous, she was — how — Andy was by it.

   (A) aware of . . amused
   (B) surprised at . . offended
   (C) disappointed by . . surprised
   (D) oblivious to . . affected
   (E) pleased about . . shocked

3. Mike is so committed to partisan politics that he — learns anything about any candidate outside his own party.

   (A) usually
   (B) always
   (C) never
   (D) consistently
   (E) occasionally

4. ENORMITY : WICKED : :

   (A) volume : loud
   (B) nurse : soothing
   (C) calamity : destructive
   (D) weight : dense
   (E) moisture : saturated

5. From the evidence in the aftermath, authorities determined that the explosion was not premeditated, but rather a/an — disruption, and so dealt with those responsible — harshly.

   (A) planned . . equally
   (B) accidental . . less
   (C) careless . . more
   (D) foolish . . particularly
   (E) organized . . somewhat

Book 7, Lesson 13 Test

Find a SYNONYM for each underlined word. Circle the letter of your answer.

1. Woodworking classes were a/an <u>adjunct</u> to the mill's main business of selling lumber.

   a distraction
   b intrusion
   c addition
   d compliment

2. The <u>carnage</u> on U.S. Civil War battlefields claimed nearly an entire generation of American soldiers.

   a destruction
   b fighting
   c sacrifices
   d memorials

3. Home gardeners are in a constant struggle to <u>eradicate</u> weeds from their lawns.

   a remove
   b relocate
   c suppress
   d clone

4. John Brown's <u>insurrection</u> began and ended with the raid of the armory at Harper's Ferry.

   a crusade
   b campaign
   c demonstration
   d revolt

5. Edgar Allan Poe is <u>singular</u> among American writers.

   a famous
   b popular
   c exceptional
   d mediocre

Find an ANTONYM for each underlined word. Circle the letter of your answer.

6. Her smile <u>belied</u> the ill will in her words.

   a supported
   b hid
   c revealed
   d contradicted

7. My neighborhood's <u>diversity</u> is evinced by the large number of nearby restaurants with food from different countries.

   a uniformity
   b variety
   c population
   d ethnicity

8. Bob was a notorious troublemaker who would <u>foment</u> a lunchtime food fight whenever he felt the conditions were ripe.

   a rouse
   b instigate
   c suppress
   d start

9. Some students feel that it is wise to take <u>mandatory</u> courses as soon as possible, while others are in no hurry to complete them.

   a elective
   b required
   c elementary
   d necessary

10. The swaying of the hammock and the crash of the surf made Yolanda particularly <u>somnolent</u>.

   a peaceful
   b distracting
   c soothing
   d stimulating

Choose the BEST way to complete each sentence or answer each question. Circle the letter of your answer.

11. A <u>dilemma</u> is what sort of problem?

    a   unusual
    b   simple
    c   difficult
    d   routine

12. To <u>flout</u> convention involves all of the following except which?

    a   reverence
    b   ignoring
    c   scorn
    d   disrespect

13. A <u>pretext</u> does what to true motives?

    a   supports them
    b   disguises them
    c   justifies them
    d   confuses them

14. Which of the following refers to the <u>singular</u>?

    a   me
    b   us
    c   they
    d   them

15. Which of the following is least likely to describe something that is <u>stalwart</u>?

    a   flimsy
    b   strong
    c   tall
    d   sturdy

SAT Sneak Preview

1. DIVERSE : VARIOUS : :

    (A) many : different
    (B) solitary : lonely
    (C) popular : friendly
    (D) uniform : same
    (E) numerous : scarce

2. Rather than flout convention, Heath removed his — and covered his — when visiting his grandparents.

    (A) earrings . . tattoos
    (B) jacket . . head
    (C) shoes . . mouth
    (D) hat . . eyes
    (E) pager . . arms

3. MITIGATE : ALLEVIATE : :

    (A) sleep : relax
    (B) aim : target
    (C) muffle : quiet
    (D) buffer : interfere
    (E) focus : intensify

4. Claire tried to reduce the somnolent effects of the lecturer's monotone voice by having a large cup of — before class.

    (A) coffee
    (B) milk
    (C) water
    (D) juice
    (E) soup

5. By convincing everyone to spay and neuter their —, the ASPCA, a stalwart supporter of animal rights, hopes to eradicate the practice of — unwanted animals.

    (A) dogs . . adopting
    (B) neighbors . . abandoning
    (C) pets . . destroying
    (D) cats . . enjoying
    (E) yards . . donating

Book 7, Lesson 14 Test

Find a SYNONYM for each underlined word. Circle the letter of your answer.

1. Smiles of <u>celestial</u> pleasure danced across the children's lips as they tasted the pastries.

   a   quiet

   b   satisfied

   c   mundane

   d   divine

2. A <u>galaxy</u> of the state's most powerful businesspeople turned out for the opening of the new state arts complex.

   a   representation

   b   group

   c   cross-section

   d   handful

3. Daniel decided to wait for an appropriate <u>juncture</u> before asking his mother if he could borrow the car on Saturday.

   a   moment

   b   location

   c   mood

   d   conversation

4. Charybdis is a <u>maelstrom</u> in Homer's epic *The Odyssey* that threatens the hero on his journey home.

   a   wizard

   b   whirlpool

   c   dragon

   d   enchantress

5. Ted Turner is a/an <u>titan</u> of mass media.

   a genius

   b pawn

   c employee

   d giant

Find an ANTONYM for each underlined word. Circle the letter of your answer.

6. To reach my house, turn right at the <u>juncture</u> of MLK and Congress, then continue three more blocks.

   a intersection

   b corner

   c separation

   d joining

7. Community newspapers in languages other than English have <u>proliferated</u> in the U.S. in recent years.

   a decreased

   b multiplied

   c appeared

   d grown

8. Warm, damp environments provide <u>optimum</u> conditions for mold to grow.

   a ideal

   b impossible

   c unlikely

   d possible

9. The legislature <u>pilloried</u> their fellow representative for claiming to work for the people, then not participating in an important vote because he was on vacation.

   a praised

   b lampooned

   c admonished

   d admired

10. You can see the resemblance if you <u>juxtapose</u> the photos of my mother and my niece.

    a   separate

    b   overlap

    c   compare

    d   inspect

Choose the BEST way to complete each sentence or answer each question. Circle the letter of your answer.

11. An <u>aberration</u> in a lens refers to its inability to do what?

    a   magnify

    b   reflect

    c   refract

    d   focus

12. Which of the following are not likely to be found in a <u>galaxy</u>?

    a   stars

    b   moons

    c   planets

    d   universes

13. A <u>juxtaposition</u> involves things arranged how?

    a   in a pile

    b   side-by-side

    c   chronologically

    d   alphabetically

14. A <u>proliferation</u> describes something that has done all of the following except what?

    a   reduced

    b   grown

    c   expanded

    d   multiplied

15. Which of the following is least likely to be described as <u>titanic</u>?

   a   a panda

   b   a gnat

   c   a whale

   d   an elephant

SAT Sneak Preview

1. ANTIQUATED : TELEGRAPH : :

   (A) modern : cellular phone

   (B) valuable : artifact

   (C) current : typewriter

   (D) relevant : computer

   (E) novelty : postcard

2. Helene was less interested in celestial affairs and more concerned with — matters.

   (A) astronomical

   (B) budgetary

   (C) humanistic

   (D) earthly

   (E) literary

3. Suki was so — with her grandfather's habits that she could say with certitude that he would be golfing until 3:00.

   (A) impressed

   (B) familiar

   (C) confused

   (D) bored

   (E) preoccupied

4. The maelstrom of — at the zoning meeting made it seem that the — had become intractable.

   (A) snacks . . afternoon

   (B) cooperation . . hearing

   (C) compliments . . discussion

   (D) insults . . gathering

   (E) arguments . . debate

5. The teaching assistants were — to learn that the financial aid office had been remiss in disbursing their —.

   (A) unhappy . . bills
   (B) thrilled . . checks
   (C) disgruntled . . stipends
   (D) surprised . . schedules
   (E) angry . . assignments

Book 7, Lesson 15 Test

Find a SYNONYM for each underlined word. Circle the letter of your answer.

1. Sharonda <u>abominated</u> the ills of society, so she found it uplifting to work actively to resolve them.

   a complained about

   b disliked

   c hated

   d ignored

2. Mr. Voelkel suggested that I <u>abridge</u> my sixty-page report to a more readable length.

   a shorten

   b extend

   c annotate

   d pad

3. Erica felt the day was off to an <u>auspicious</u> start when she awoke before the alarm and was early to work.

   a ominous

   b shaky

   c promising

   d unbelievable

4. A small band of defenders inside the Alamo were <u>beleaguered</u> by General Santa Ana's army for almost two weeks in 1836.

   a beaten

   b surrounded

   c threatened

   d admired

5. Health care professionals <u>inveigh</u> against the disappearing physical education curriculum in public schools.

   a protest

   b vote

   c advise

   d warn

Find an ANTONYM for each underlined word. Circle the letter of your answer.

6. Because of her <u>abominable</u> reputation as an impossible perfectionist, students did their best to avoid taking Dr. Villaume's composition class.

   a lovable

   b detestable

   c loathsome

   d undeserved

7. Despite their rivalry during baseball season, no <u>animosity</u> remains between fans of the teams during the off-season.

   a rancor

   b hostility

   c cooperation

   d fondness

8. Mutineers <u>sabotaged</u> navigational charts so the captain would be unsure of where they were last seen.

   a repaired

   b damaged

   c destroyed

   d highlighted

9. The <u>sadistic</u> drill sergeant thought it toughened the troops to restrict their access to water while working out in the hot sun for hours.

   a cruel

   b compassionate

   c dangerous

   d thoughtful

10. It <u>transpired</u> that the physics substitute was an impostor who knew nothing about the subject at all.

    a   emerged

    b   turned out

    c   happened

    d   was rumored

Choose the BEST way to complete each sentence or answer each question. Circle the letter of your answer.

11. Which of the following is most likely to <u>beleaguer</u> a blood drive?

    a   fear of needles

    b   plenty of beds

    c   trained nurses

    d   tempting snacks

12. What does a <u>confidante</u> know?

    a   history

    b   trivia

    c   secrets

    d   passwords

13. How would a director probably feel about a <u>scathing</u> review?

    a   smug

    b   flattered

    c   hurt

    d   elated

14. Which of the following is least related to something that has <u>transpired</u>?

    a   happened

    b   occurred

    c   past

    d   idea

15. If you have to <u>inure</u> yourself to something, it is probably

    a   unpleasant

    b   unusual

    c   foreign

    d   desirable

SAT Sneak Preview

1. ABOMINABLE : CRUELTY : :

    (A) repulsive : sorrow

    (B) offensive : rudeness

    (C) terrible : greatness

    (D) hopeful : kindness

    (E) attractive : optimism

2. Although the original version of *The Odyssey* has much more detail, the abridged version is —.

    (A) older

    (B) bigger

    (C) thicker

    (D) heavier

    (E) lighter

3. The mayor often — her constituents, and is more popular than her predecessor, who — talked to townspeople.

    (A) meets with . . rarely

    (B) refers to . . often

    (C) discusses . . sometimes

    (D) listens to . . constantly

    (E) thanks . . regularly

4. Although for generations pledges had inured themselves to — hazing rituals to get into a fraternity, the iniquitous practice has been — on many college campuses today.

    (A) harmless . . reintroduced

    (B) silly . . encouraged

    (C) dangerous . . banned

    (D) humiliating . . traditional

    (E) thoughtless . . renewed

5. SABOTAGE : INTENTIONAL : :

   (A) damage : destructive
   (B) accident : unplanned
   (C) mistake : designed
   (D) joke : constructive
   (E) misfortune : lucky

Book 7, Lesson 16 Test

Find a SYNONYM for each underlined word. Circle the letter of your answer.

1. Laura has a/an <u>aura</u> of serenity, no matter what the circumstance.

   a manner
   b mood
   c expression
   d atmosphere

2. The professor outlined the functions for the class activities and website, but it was up to the <u>factotum</u> to make them a reality.

   a students
   b assistant
   c parents
   d administration

3. The <u>grandiose</u> manor ballroom dwarfed the small group of sightseers.

   a huge
   b gaudy
   c ornate
   d cozy

4. His outspoken, outdated <u>intransigence</u> on the issue of women's professional equality made Ross an easy target for his sister's scorn.

   a rants
   b stubbornness
   c jokes
   d chauvinism

5. Knowing when to ignore <u>picayune</u> details is what separates the good reporters from the great ones.

   a small
   b boring
   c sordid
   d insignificant

Find an ANTONYM for each underlined word. Circle the letter of your answer.

6. The tourists were <u>bemused</u> by the early-morning flurry of activity at the bed and breakfast, which was also a working farm.

   a   soothed
   b   bewildered
   c   awakened
   d   confused

7. Without looking behind her, Kendra was <u>cognizant</u> that someone had just entered the room.

   a   suspicious
   b   afraid
   c   mindful
   d   unaware

8. In the event that a child consumes a poisonous substance, you should always call the poison control center before you <u>induce</u> vomiting in the child.

   a   trigger
   b   start
   c   stop
   d   interfere

9. The administration remained <u>intransigent</u> on the issue of allowing students to leave campus during their lunch hour.

   a   closed-minded
   b   flexible
   c   uncompromising
   d   supportive

10. Jeri arranged flowers into bouquets with such <u>panache</u> that onlookers were fooled into thinking it was easy.

    a   flair
    b   care
    c   awkwardness
    d   dash

Choose the BEST way to complete each sentence or answer each question. Circle the letter of your answer.

11. What does a <u>conundrum</u> sometimes involve?

    a   a sight gag

    b   an insult

    c   a play on words

    d   a practical joke

12. A <u>grandiose</u> claim is least likely to be which of the following?

    a   pretentious

    b   exaggerated

    c   absurd

    d   modest

13. A <u>promontory</u> is a good place for what?

    a   a library

    b   a mailbox

    c   a runway

    d   a lighthouse

14. What effect is a <u>banal</u> book most likely to have on its reader?

    a   boredom

    b   delight

    c   suspense

    d   disgust

15. Which of the following most describes an <u>evanescent</u> event?

    a   temporary

    b   endless

    c   surreal

    d   awe-inspiring

SAT Sneak Preview

1. BANAL : ORIGINAL : :

    (A) predictable : obvious
    (B) trite : fresh
    (C) surprising : unexpected
    (D) boring : common
    (E) interesting : curious

2. It was a conundrum to us that Drew never seemed to — but always made perfect grades.

    (A) study
    (B) worry
    (C) relax
    (D) rest
    (E) listen

3. EVANESCENT : ENDURING : :

    (A) illuminated : intermittent
    (B) painful : necessary
    (C) fleeting : ephemeral
    (D) fragile : solid
    (E) temporary : permanent

4. The laudatory reviews and — shows induced the quartet to — their concert dates in our town.

    (A) packed . . extend
    (B) empty . . renew
    (C) popular . . delay
    (D) crowded . . shorten
    (E) unpopular . . drop

5. Since she had a predilection for cold-blooded creatures, Kari was — the reptile exhibit.

    (A) afraid of
    (B) uninterested in
    (C) fascinated by
    (D) cautious about
    (E) ambivalent toward

Book 7, Lesson 17 Test

Find a SYNONYM for each underlined word. Circle the letter of your answer.

1. When he looked at his <u>aggregate</u> clothing expenditures for the year, Charles had to admit that he had an obsession with fashion.

   a biggest

   b smallest

   c average

   d total

2. Alanna <u>allocated</u> the hours right after school for homework.

   a set aside

   b intended

   c distributed

   d wanted

3. Engineering, though hardly the <u>bastion</u> it once was, is still predominantly populated by men.

   a island

   b stronghold

   c arena

   d vehicle

4. Marianne <u>importuned</u> Susan to take over her babysitting job Friday night.

   a nominated

   b pleaded for

   c suggested

   d forbade

5. The class spent days <u>ruminating</u> over the meaning of Toni Morrison's novel *Sula*.

   a pondering

   b debating

   c arguing

   d deliberating

Find an ANTONYM for each underlined word. Circle the letter of your answer.

6. The buzz around town <u>augurs</u> the success of the new vegetarian restaurant.

   a   guarantees
   b   promises
   c   casts doubt upon
   d   bodes well for

7. Though Yvette's files were in complete <u>disarray</u>, she seemed to know where everything was instantly.

   a   order
   b   confusion
   c   chaos
   d   categories

8. The Real Estate Commission has no <u>jurisdiction</u> over lenders.

   a   reach
   b   control
   c   authority
   d   powerlessness

9. Tanya found comfort in her <u>ruminations</u> about loss after her dog died.

   a   reflections
   b   thoughts
   c   actions
   d   ideas

10. Martin showed great <u>temerity</u> when he corrected the professor's math in front of the class.

   a   boldness
   b   timidity
   c   stupidity
   d   impulsiveness

Choose the BEST way to complete each sentence or answer each question. Circle the letter of your answer.

11. To <u>allocate</u> resources means to distribute them according to what?

    a a whim
    b a lottery
    c a plan
    d a schedule

12. Which of the following is most likely to be described as a <u>bastion</u>?

    a a fortress
    b a playground
    c a jungle
    d an igloo

13. Which of the following descriptions of Geoff is probably not <u>hyperbole</u>?

    a He's as strong as an ox.
    b He's as stubborn as a mule.
    c He's as poor as a church mouse.
    d He's as smart as his brother.

14. <u>Decorum</u> refers to behavior that is which of the following?

    a proper
    b entertaining
    c risky
    d humble

15. A <u>halcyon</u> environment is least likely to make you feel

    a peaceful.
    b lucky.
    c anxious.
    d bored.

SAT Sneak Preview

1. The art director considered the aggregate of the staff's work on the ad campaign, winnowed the most — from the rest, and sent only the — to the client.

   (A) difficult . . worst
   (B) boring . . prettiest
   (C) inspiring . . dullest
   (D) flashy . . smallest
   (E) creative . . best

2. AUGUR : FUTURE : :

   (A) fear : omen
   (B) reminisce : past
   (C) evince : present
   (D) inherit : heir
   (E) record : history

3. We will — the recently defunct ice cream delivery service when we are feeling lazy on a hot summer night.

   (A) miss
   (B) duplicate
   (C) replace
   (D) regret
   (E) restore

4. HALCYON : AGITATED : :

   (A) happy : garrulous
   (B) tense : anxious
   (C) peaceful : drowsy
   (D) upset : calm
   (E) educated : prosperous

5. Believing that — reflect(s) —, Aunt Iva often delivered homilies to her nephews when they displayed a lack of decorum.

   (A) behaviors . . personality
   (B) experiences . . strength
   (C) politeness . . pleasantness
   (D) manners . . morals
   (E) offenses . . outrageousness

Book 7, Lesson 18 Test

Find a SYNONYM for each underlined word. Circle the letter of your answer.

1. The <u>assemblage</u> at World Youth Day included students from the six inhabited continents.

    a   participants

    b   delegates

    c   ambassadors

    d   gathering

2. Kamilla and Ronnie enjoyed <u>caviling</u> about obscure points of civil law.

    a   quibbling

    b   joking

    c   screaming

    d   betting

3. There are only five <u>extant</u> copies of the Gutenberg Bible in the U.S.

    a   partial

    b   existing

    c   remnant

    d   priceless

4. Michael Jordan is considered basketball's <u>nonpareil</u> icon.

    a   modern

    b   timeless

    c   unequaled

    d   purest

5. After decades under Mabel's care, the bedroom furniture had developed an enviable <u>patina</u>.

    a   finish

    b   value

    c   distress

    d   age

Find an ANTONYM for each underlined word. Circle the letter of your answer.

6. Government is not a single entity, but a/an <u>assemblage</u> of many organizations.

   a   system
   b   separation
   c   series
   d   bureaucracy

7. Maid Marian felt safe in Sherwood Forest when she was traveling under the <u>auspices</u> of the king.

   a   protection
   b   support
   c   patronage
   d   opposition

8. Shannon was happy to do her holiday shopping with Heather, the <u>nonpareil</u> of gift-givers.

   a   champion
   b   expert
   c   worst
   d   norm

9. The campers' <u>rapt</u> expressions showed their feelings about the campfire ghost stories.

   a   displeased
   b   engrossed
   c   bored
   d   hesitant

10. Hank tried to <u>resuscitate</u> interest in his fledgling market research company by sending a free report to industry press outlets.

   a   renew
   b   generate
   c   destroy
   d   increase

Choose the BEST way to complete each sentence or answer each question. Circle the letter of your answer.

11. <u>Acoustic</u> relates most to which of the following?

    a hearing
    b sight
    c smell
    d taste

12. Which of the following is an <u>august</u> person least likely to inspire?

    a respect
    b admiration
    c awe
    d disapproval

13. A <u>cavil</u> is what sort of concern?

    a health
    b legal
    c major
    d minor

14. When copper develops a <u>patina</u>, what color does it turn?

    a black
    b gold
    c green
    d gray

15. What does a <u>rapt</u> expression display?

    a attention
    b pleasure
    c anguish
    d surprise

SAT Sneak Preview

1. The concert hall's superb acoustics — the singer's mellifluous —.

   (A) disguised . . figure
   (B) muffled . . lyrics
   (C) disguised . . dress
   (D) enhanced . . voice
   (E) amplified . . fans

2. CURATOR : MUSEUM : :

   (A) grocer : apples
   (B) teacher : classroom
   (C) operator : telephone
   (D) actor : movie
   (E) gourmet : pots

3. The drama evoked emotions running the gamut from — to despair.

   (A) regret
   (B) hopelessness
   (C) sadness
   (D) depression
   (E) joy

4. With his — mien, you would never guess the ineffable — the groundskeeper had made to the college over the years.

   (A) humble . . contributions
   (B) extravagant . . donations
   (C) lazy . . charges
   (D) timid . . boasts
   (E) serious . . lessons

5. Jessica tried to resuscitate her — design business by introducing trendy new styles.

   (A) successful
   (B) popular
   (C) failing
   (D) profitable
   (E) expensive

Book 7, Lesson 19 Test

Find a SYNONYM for each underlined word. Circle the letter of your answer.

1. "I only regret that I have but one life to lose for my country" is a quote <u>ascribed</u> to Revolutionary War hero Nathan Hale.

   a credited
   b known
   c particular
   d attributed

2. It is hard to stay angry at someone with as much <u>ebullience</u> as Carson.

   a charm
   b personality
   c money
   d enthusiasm

3. Sailors believe that a red sky at night is a <u>harbinger</u> of clear sailing.

   a herald
   b fortune
   c superstition
   d myth

4. The <u>homogeneity</u> of the batter shows that the fruit and nuts have been evenly distributed throughout it.

   a unevenness
   b combination
   c uniformity
   d a selection

5. The <u>incumbent</u> president is trying to get elected to another term.

   a former
   b current
   c aspiring
   d popular

Find an ANTONYM for each underlined word. Circle the letter of your answer.

6. Never having visited the city before, Pam was <u>amenable</u> to/for suggestions about good restaurants for breakfast.

   a hostile

   b agreeable

   c eager

   d ambivalent

7. Holly's <u>ebullient</u> personality can be tiresome sometimes.

   a bubbly

   b dark

   c cheerful

   d bright

8. Though he wasn't helping the agenda progress, Barry's <u>fatuous</u> comments were at least helping to keep the mood light.

   a weighty

   b foolish

   c unrelated

   d confusing

9. The student body is not very <u>homogeneous</u>, with nearly a third speaking a native language other than English.

   a uniform

   b similar

   c interesting

   d diverse

10. Doug is fascinated by naming conventions in <u>matriarchal</u> societies.

    a democratic

    b male-dominated

    c solitary

    d female-governed

Choose the BEST way to complete each sentence or answer each question. Circle the letter of your answer.

11. Which of the following people is least likely to want to be described as <u>charismatic</u>?

    a   movie star
    b   politician
    c   talk show host
    d   inventor

12. An <u>entrepreneur</u> does what to a business?

    a   audits it
    b   advises it
    c   assumes the risk
    d   lends it money

13. Which of the following is least related to an <u>incumbent</u>?

    a   occupant
    b   position
    c   future
    d   office

14. A <u>matriarchy</u> refers to a society headed by what?

    a   mothers
    b   females
    c   fathers
    d   males

15. Which of the following best describes a <u>prerogative</u>?

    a   choice
    b   preference
    c   privilege
    d   alternative

SAT Sneak Preview

1. DEARTH : DROUGHT : :

    (A) glut : shortage
    (B) scarcity : heap
    (C) need : thirst
    (D) abundance : flood
    (E) gift : endowment

2. The squad was demoralized after doing very — at the regional competition, so they were amenable to outside —.

    (A) poorly . . advice
    (B) well . . instruction
    (C) splendidly . . participation
    (D) roughly . . influences
    (E) smoothly . . praise

3. As head of the blood drive committee, it is incumbent upon Sean to publicize the event to — donations.

    (A) reduce
    (B) maximize
    (C) persuade
    (D) minimize
    (E) suppress

4. NEOPHYTE : EXPERT : :

    (A) student : graduate
    (B) manager : retiree
    (C) beginner : professional
    (D) infant : teenager
    (E) seeker : mentor

5. Although they have the same —, Dawn and Gordon are not siblings.

    (A) hair color
    (B) schedule
    (C) address
    (D) hobbies
    (E) last name

Book 7, Lesson 20 Test

Find a SYNONYM for each underlined word. Circle the letter of your answer.

1. Ben tried to <u>bilk</u> the cable company out of its fees by removing the filter from his line.

   a cheat

   b talk

   c trick

   d challenge

2. The guide was <u>conversant</u> with/to local plants, and could reassure Sara that the patch she fell into was not poison ivy.

   a allergic

   b accustomed

   c familiar

   d attached

3. It was <u>fortuitous</u> that Todd was home from school sick on the day that his father locked his keys in his car.

   a unfortunate

   b lucky

   c coincidental

   d awkward

4. Rosario's allergies were severe, and even a <u>miniscule</u> amount of peanut would cause a reaction.

   a tiny

   b reasonable

   c standard

   d large

5. Jackson came to believe that there was some <u>stigma</u> attached to his hobby of collecting cockroaches.

   a challenges

   b status

   c shame

   d benefits

Find an ANTONYM for each underlined word. Circle the letter of your answer.

6. For the first time ever, the school year ended without the yearbook project's being <u>consummated</u>.

   a started

   b finished

   c billed

   d distributed

7. Diane's <u>credulity</u> made her a favorite target for Mel's practical jokes.

   a sophistication

   b gullibility

   c innocence

   d skepticism

8. After surviving on a raft for days with just water and bread, the castaways greeted the meal of steak, potatoes, and chocolate cake with <u>euphoria</u>.

   a elation

   b joy

   c despair

   d suspicion

9. She left me a message so <u>incoherent</u> that I almost didn't understand that she needed a ride from the airport.

   a straightforward

   b rambling

   c long

   d confusing

10. Chad was in the habit of <u>procrastinating</u> on assignments when he felt panic about approaching deadlines.

   a delaying

   b starting

   c working

   d meditating

Choose the BEST way to complete each sentence or answer each question. Circle the letter of your answer.

11. Someone who is <u>credulous</u> is easily

   a bored.

   b frightened.

   c convinced.

   d bribed.

12. A <u>hypothetical</u> question is least likely to be which of the following?

   a supposed

   b imagined

   c genuine

   d assumed

13. <u>Incoherence</u> deals with things that are difficult to

   a accept.

   b prove.

   c believe.

   d understand.

14. When people exchange <u>pleasantries</u>, what do they trade?

   a business cards

   b small gifts

   c casual remarks

   d minor favors

15. Which of the following is most related to <u>stigmatizing</u> something?

   a   a place of honor
   b   a bad name
   c   a scornful look
   d   a handout

SAT Sneak Preview

1. ACCOST : AGGRESSIVE : :

   (A) salute : respectful
   (B) confront : rude
   (C) approach : demanding
   (D) challenge : cowardly
   (E) elude : soft

2. Although he started the day in a — mood, Dylan became euphoric after his fortuitous — with his idol in the grocery store.

   (A) jubilant . . appointment
   (B) fanciful . . meeting
   (C) gloomy . . encounter
   (D) anxious . . collision
   (E) aggressive . . schedule

3. AVARICE : WEALTH : :

   (A) despair : violence
   (B) pride : ego
   (C) blanket : cold
   (D) water : drink
   (E) starvation : food

4. Although I can't — it, I have a hypothesis that left-handed people are more sociable.

   (A) admit
   (B) prove
   (C) report
   (D) discuss
   (E) patent

5. Austin had always been a fast —, and he had no qualms about procrastinating about the start of major projects —.

   (A) worker . . until the last minute
   (B) talker . . immediately
   (C) thinker . . as soon as possible
   (D) runner . . at night
   (E) learner . . on the weekends

Book 7, Final Test 1 (Lessons 1–20)

Read the passage. Choose the BEST answer for each sentence or question about an underlined word. Circle the letter of your answer.

NATURE'S FURY

In the summer of A.D. 79, a <u>cataclysmic</u> eruption of the volcano Mt. Vesuvius, probably the deadliest eruption ever, destroyed the 500-year-old city of Pompeii, in southern Italy. It was a resort town where wealthy Romans were able to relax and enjoy the beautiful landscape near the Amalfi coast. It is now a snapshot, frozen in time, of life at the height of the Roman Empire.

History had forgotten Pompeii altogether until it was rediscovered in 1748. The excavation began immediately and continues to this day. About 200 skeletons of those who died that day have been discovered, <u>interred</u> where they fell, their forms preserved in ash. The agonized faces of those unfortunate people have been recovered by making plaster casts of the hollows left in the hardened ash after their bodies decomposed; in this way, the dead can tell their story to <u>posterity</u>. As the perfectly preserved city, its artifacts, and the forms of its inhabitants were unearthed, the story of life in the ancient Italian resort town <u>materialized</u>. It was a <u>grandiose</u> city with luxurious homes that featured gardens, running water for private baths, and decorative mosaics and painted stucco. A <u>proliferation</u> of amenities has also been uncovered, including sidewalks, waterworks, a thriving woolen industry, bakeries, restaurants, and entertainment in the form of sports and theater.

The town was still rebuilding from a violent earthquake 17 years earlier when it was destroyed as Vesuvius sprang to life. The volcano had given <u>acoustic</u> foreshadowings for days, but the veterans of life in the shadow of the volcano were unworried. There had been time to escape, but the residents were not <u>cognizant</u> of the danger so they did not heed the warnings. They never dreamed the volcano could erupt with such <u>enormity</u>. In less than two days, the town was buried more than 20 feet deep in rock and ash. Pompeii was not the only victim of Vesuvius's power. The villas at Stabiae and the nearby town of Herculaneum were also wiped out.

An eyewitness account of the catastrophe was provided by Pliny the Younger, who was visiting his uncle, Pliny the Elder, at the time. He watched the horror from across the Bay of Naples and wrote of it in letters to a friend. Those letters paint a clear picture of what transpired. He described what is now called a "Plinian" event, when an explosive eruption shoots volcanic material high into the air and blankets a large area with ash. Pliny the Younger also described how his uncle, commander of the Roman fleet at Misenum, died leading a rescue mission over the bay.

Archaeological evidence shows that Pompeii's residents thought the initial shower of ash was the end of Vesuvius's aberration, and returned to their homes before the first of three deadly, lightning-fast avalanches of boiling mud, gas, and debris started. Moving at a rate of about one mile per minute, the flows beset Pompeii and suffocated anyone unfortunate enough to be in their path. In less than a day, Vesuvius had claimed some 16,000 lives.

It was not the first time the mountain exploded, nor was it the last. There is evidence of eruptions as early as the sixth century B.C. and as recent as 1944, with experts expecting another within a decade or two. Despite history's lesson, about three million people currently live in the area that would be affected by another large eruption.

1. Which of the following is most likely to be described as cataclysmic?

   a a race car
   b an airplane
   c a storm
   d an earthquake

2. As used in the second paragraph, interred most closely means

   a buried.
   b coiled.
   c hidden.
   d damaged.

3. As used in paragraph two, materialized means

   a vanished.
   b moved.
   c appeared.
   d expanded.

4. A person who is <u>grandiose</u> is most likely to be

   a   extravagant.
   b   modest.
   c   beautiful.
   d   funny.

5. <u>Proliferation</u>, as used in paragraph two, most closely means

   a   variety.
   b   shortage.
   c   abundance.
   d   group.

6. Which of the following is least related to the word <u>enormity</u>, as used in paragraph three?

   a   severity
   b   rage
   c   strength
   d   insignificance

7. The word <u>aberration</u> describes things that are

   a   unusual.
   b   scary.
   c   timely.
   d   common.

8. Which of the following is a synonym for <u>beset</u>?

   a   bewilder
   b   attack
   c   worry
   d   interest

9. As used in the selection, <u>posterity</u> deals mainly with

   a   past.
   b   future.
   c   present.
   d   history.

10. All of the following are synonyms for <u>transpire</u> (as used in the fourth paragraph) except

   a   occur.
   b   exist.
   c   happen.
   d   take place.

SAT Sneak Preview

1. As used in the third paragraph, <u>cognizant</u> most nearly means

   (A) sensitive
   (B) restless
   (C) worried
   (D) upset
   (E) aware

2. <u>Acoustic</u> is most closely related to

   (A) sight
   (B) sound
   (C) smell
   (D) touch
   (E) taste

3. Which of the following is least likely to be considered <u>grandiose</u>?

   (A) a cottage
   (B) a skyscraper
   (C) a palace
   (D) a ballroom
   (E) a yacht

4. As used in the third paragraph, <u>enormity</u> is most closely related to the state of being

   (A) average
   (B) rare
   (C) special
   (D) scary
   (E) monstrous

5. An antonym for <u>cataclysmic</u> is

    (A) sudden

    (B) catastrophic

    (C) gentle

    (D) violent

    (E) fabled

Book 7, Final Test 2 (Lessons 1–20)

Read the passage. Choose the BEST answer for each sentence or question about an underlined word. Circle the letter of your answer.

BENJAMIN FRANKLIN:
PRINTER, INVENTOR, STATESMAN, AMERICAN

Benjamin Franklin was born in Boston in 1706, the fifteenth of seventeen children. With only two years of formal education, he was working with his father at candlemaking by the age of ten. By age twelve, he was apprenticed to his brother James, a printer. He began writing essays anonymously for publication in his brother's newspaper when he was still a teenager. By his early twenties, Franklin had his own printing business in Philadelphia. Believing that the difference between success and failure was a little hard work, Franklin usually arrived at work earlier and stayed later than his neighbors. That hard work would make it possible for him to spend the second half of his life working to improve the lives of all Americans.

A self-educated man, he had a way with both the spoken and written word. He did not write in a grandiloquent manner, preferring a colloquial style more accessible to ordinary people. His newspaper, *The Pennsylvania Gazette*, and his annual *Poor Richard's Almanack* were very popular and successful among Philadelphians, due in large part to his articles. During this time he penned many an axiom familiar to us all today, including "a penny saved is a penny earned," "time is money," and "an apple a day keeps the doctor away." In face-to-face interaction, he was quick with a gibe to get a laugh. Thomas Jefferson reportedly said that the reason Franklin was not allowed to write the whole Declaration of Independence was that he would have included too many jokes.

His political career started in his thirtieth year, when he was elected clerk of the state legislature. He became postmaster of Pennsylvania the following year. He made improvements in mail delivery, civil defense, and firefighting, and he established the first public library during this time. By his early forties, his success as a printing entrepreneur afforded him an early retirement where he could focus on his diverse interests. He performed numerous experiments with electricity and invented the lightning rod. His other inventions and ideas included bifocal glasses, the odometer, the Franklin stove, daylight savings time, and the political cartoon. He invented things for the betterment of humankind and refused to patent them or accept any recompense for them.

A consummate statesman, he spent the years from 1765 to 1775 in England working to promote the cause of colonial rights. He saw that relations between England and the colonies were becoming more tense, and returned to his home just as the American Revolution started. The next year, at the age of seventy-one, he was sent to France to muster support for a treaty between France and the American colonies. He remained in France for nine years. The rustic American was very charismatic, the object of much adulation in his new home. He became a hero to the French, and he enjoyed his later years in the company of diplomats and nobility. The French placed his portrait on everything from chamber pots to snuffboxes. Nearly eighty years old when he made his final voyage to Philadelphia, and ailing from the effects of old age, Franklin was carried into Independence Hall to help draft the U.S. Constitution in 1787. He spent the last year of his life bedridden and he died in 1790, but not before writing an article denouncing American slavery. The assemblage at his funeral was about 20,000 people, all turned out to pay their final respects to a true American hero.

1. Which of the following is an antonym for grandiloquent?

   a formal
   b hasty
   c humble
   d arrogant

2. Colloquial, as used in the second paragraph, most closely means

   a simple.
   b proper.
   c smooth.
   d informal.

3. As used in the fourth paragraph, charismatic most closely means

   a boring.
   b charming.
   c rude.
   d respectful.

4. An antonym for consummate, as used in the fourth paragraph, is

   a concerned.
   b incompetent.
   c natural.
   d accomplished.

5. Which of the following words also means <u>assemblage</u>?

   a   bouquet
   b   crowd
   c   buffet
   d   mourners

6. A synonym for <u>gibe</u>, as used in the second paragraph, is

   a   joke.
   b   story.
   c   swindle.
   d   answer.

7. Which of the following is a synonym for <u>axiom</u>?

   a   song
   b   phrase
   c   principle
   d   poem

8. Which of the following people is least likely to be an <u>entrepreneur</u>?

   a   baker
   b   inventor
   c   receptionist
   d   tailor

9. As used in paragraph three, <u>diverse</u> means

   a   various.
   b   similar.
   c   difficult.
   d   obscure.

10. A synonym for <u>recompense</u> is

   a   award.
   b   praise.
   c   compensation.
   d   criticism.

SAT Sneak Preview

1. In the last paragraph, <u>adulation</u> most nearly means

   (A) admiration

   (B) conversation

   (C) debate

   (D) love

   (E) ridicule

2. As used in the selection, <u>muster</u> most nearly means

   (A) preach

   (B) earn

   (C) promise

   (D) encourage

   (E) gather

3. The word <u>consummate</u>, as used in paragraph four, most closely means

   (A) educated

   (B) funny

   (C) skilled

   (D) foreign

   (E) ordinary

4. A synonym for <u>grandiloquent</u> is

   (A) pompous

   (B) inconsiderate

   (C) modest

   (D) foolish

   (E) proud

5. For which of the following are you most likely to receive <u>recompense</u>?

   (A) a favor

   (B) an assignment

   (C) a gift

   (D) a job

   (E) a punishment

Book 7, Final Test 3 (Lessons 1–20)

Read the passage. Choose the BEST answer for each sentence or question about an underlined word. Circle the letter of your answer.

LIBERTY ENLIGHTENING THE WORLD

The Statue of Liberty has welcomed travelers to New York Harbor since 1886. Reaching more than three hundred feet above the water atop her pedestal, she makes an impressive sight for any visitor. For the millions who sailed into the harbor to make a new life, Lady Liberty was the first glimpse of the New World, and the effect was <u>mesmerizing</u>. To people fleeing political oppression and economic hardship, the giant statue with her torch held high was a <u>harbinger</u> of freedom and prosperity. She holds in her left hand a tablet inscribed with the date July 4, 1776. With her placid <u>countenance</u> gazing outward and the broken chains of tyranny at her feet, she embodies the <u>inalienable</u> rights described in the Declaration of Independence: life, liberty, and the pursuit of happiness.

"Liberty Enlightening the World," the statue's formal name, was a gift to the United States from France to commemorate the United States' <u>centennial</u>, even though construction delays kept the statue from being completed on time. French sculptor Frederic-Auguste Bartholdi, the statue's designer and champion, thought it especially timely to mark the occasion and honor the two countries' friendship at a time when France was struggling to establish its own republic. He traveled to the U.S. with a sketch, a model, and a mission to get the monument built. Ultimately, France and the U.S. decided to share the cost, with France paying for the statue and the U.S. paying for the pedestal upon which it stands. Massive fund-raising projects were <u>implemented</u> on both sides of the Atlantic to make Bartholdi's vision a reality. Even schoolchildren contributed their pennies.

Bartholdi had been impressed by the <u>aura</u> of majesty in the <u>titanic</u> monuments of Egypt. "Their kindly and impassive glance seems to ignore the present and to be fixed upon an unlimited future," he noted. The problem of how to create a structure so large, yet still light enough to be shipped across an ocean, was solved when the artist decided on a technique called repoussé, which involved copper sheets hammered into molds. The molded outer skin was fastened to a metal skeleton designed by French engineer Alexandre-Gustave Eiffel, who would be known to posterity for his famous tower in Paris. The statue arrived in New York in 1885, well behind schedule, in 214 wooden packing crates.

She was fully assembled and unveiled on October 28, 1886. The day was a public holiday, and there was a huge celebration in honor of the event. From then until 1902, the statue served as a functional luminary whose beacon shining from the torch could be seen for 24 miles. In 1901 the torch was redesigned in glass to provide even more light. By the time her lighthouse duties were behind her, the statue's copper skin had developed the patina that gives it the green color we recognize today. President Calvin Coolidge declared the Statue of Liberty to be a national monument in 1924.

In time for her own centennial in 1986, a multimillion-dollar project to refurbish the monument was launched. Time had corroded the 1,600 wrought iron bands that girded the skeleton and anchored the skin, so they were replaced by stainless steel. The torch was also restored to Bartholdi's original design, and an elevator was installed. Stronger than ever before, Lady Liberty remains poised at the gateway to the New World, ready to enlighten the world for centuries to come.

1. A synonym for mesmerizing is

   a   boring.
   b   interesting.
   c   fascinating.
   d   obvious.

2. As used in the fourth paragraph, patina means

   a   size.
   b   blemish.
   c   film.
   d   disease.

3. A harbinger is something that

   a   warns.
   b   represents.
   c   reports.
   d   foretells.

4. Which of the following would not be described as a <u>luminary</u>?

    a a cave
    b the sun
    c a lighthouse
    d a flashlight

5. As used in paragraph one, <u>inalienable</u> describes things that are

    a temporary.
    b permanent.
    c transferable.
    d negotiable.

6. As used in paragraph two, <u>centennial</u> most describes a/an

    a independence.
    b liberation.
    c freedom.
    d anniversary.

7. As used in paragraph two, <u>implemented</u> means

    a planned.
    b abandoned.
    c accomplished.
    d carried out.

8. Of the following articles of clothing, which one is most likely to <u>gird</u> as the word is used in the selection?

    a a belt
    b a sweater
    c socks
    d pants

9. As used in the third paragraph, <u>aura</u> refers to all of the following except

    a feeling.
    b smell.
    c sensation.
    d image.

10. As used in paragraph three, <u>titanic</u> refers to

   a   size.
   b   style.
   c   shape.
   d   weight.

SAT Sneak Preview

1. As used in paragraph four, <u>luminary</u> is most closely related to

   (A) inspiration
   (B) celebrity
   (C) light
   (D) shelter
   (E) power

2. To <u>refurbish</u> means to

   (A) restore
   (B) destroy
   (C) decorate
   (D) cover
   (E) clean

3. Which of the following is least likely to <u>mesmerize</u>?

   (A) a daredevil
   (B) a celebrity
   (C) a hypnotist
   (D) a grocer
   (E) a ghost

4. Which is not related to <u>countenance</u>, as used in the first paragraph?

   (A) appearance
   (B) look
   (C) face
   (D) expression
   (E) attitude

5. As used in the fifth paragraph, <u>gird</u> is least related to something that

   (A) binds
   (B) releases
   (C) supports
   (D) encircles
   (E) surrounds

Book 7, Final Test 4 (Lessons 1–20)

Read the passage. Choose the BEST answer for each sentence or question about an underlined word. Circle the letter of your answer.

THE AMERICAN "FRENCH" CHEF

Julia Child is <u>singular</u> among American chefs. She was one of the first TV chefs, and the first to deliver <u>gourmet</u> cuisine from its lofty perch into the hands of the modern home cook. From the seeds she planted grew a new way of thinking about food, a new style of cookbook, and a new kind of celebrity for chefs.

After graduating from college, living in New York in the 1930s, she couldn't even cook yet. She wanted a career as a writer, though decades would pass before she published her first book. She went to work writing advertising and publicity copy for a furniture maker. At the start of World War II, she went to Washington, D.C., to work for the Office of Strategic Services and was transferred to Ceylon (now Sri Lanka), where she met her future husband, Paul Child. Because Julia had a natural love of fine food, but not the natural ability to prepare it, she said he married her not for her ability in the kitchen, but in spite of it. A new wife at the age of 34, she decided to learn to cook. Paul's job took them to Paris, where Julia's culinary <u>odyssey</u> truly began. She became <u>infatuated</u> with French food, and studied at the world-renowned Cordon Bleu cooking school. She then began teaching in her home and working on her first cookbook, *Mastering the Art of French Cooking*, which she wrote with two other cooks. It was published ten years later, when she was 50 years old. After receiving rave reviews on her cookbook and a few television appearances, Julia was offered her own television show—the first-ever cooking show—called *The French Chef*.

Her timing was right, as after World War II many people in the U.S. had the leisure to take time to cook again, and some were later inspired by the young, charming first lady serving French cuisine at the White House. Julia's <u>charisma</u> and humor made the subject of French cooking accessible to everyone. She made mistakes and laughed at herself, and in doing so, she took the pressure off home cooks who were intimidated by complicated French techniques and rules. Teaching with explanation and example, she demystified the <u>rudiments</u> of the cuisine, such as sauces, and <u>induced</u> her followers to attempt more elaborate dishes. Whether inspiring them to <u>concoct</u> a bouillabaisse or a vinaigrette, Julia gave them the courage to begin. She was as ebullient as she was expert, and her fans tuned in every week with rapt attention.

Julia Child started a new career at an age when her peers were more likely looking toward retirement. She was a rare female presence in the male bastion that was the culinary industry. Her entrepreneurial instincts helped her stay fresh and relevant over four decades, through nine cookbooks, and with the always-evolving TV shows. She changed the way Americans cook and the way they eat. Her contributions are so influential that she has been granted an honorary degree from Harvard University, and her kitchen has been displayed at the Smithsonian's National Museum of American History. But beyond those hallowed halls, her influence is felt every day on dinner plates on dinner tables around the country.

1. As used in the first paragraph, something that is singular is least likely to be

    a   outstanding.
    b   exceptional.
    c   famous.
    d   extraordinary.

2. Where are you most likely to find gourmet food?

    a   a deli
    b   a school cafeteria
    c   a picnic
    d   a restaurant

3. As used in the fourth paragraph, a bastion is most likely to be a/an

    a   club.
    b   stronghold.
    c   association.
    d   tradition.

4. Which of the following is most closely related to ebullient, as used in the third paragraph?

    a   helpful
    b   beautiful
    c   smart
    d   enthusiastic

5. An antonym for <u>concoct</u> is

  a   destroy.

  b   prepare.

  c   create.

  d   invent.

6. Which of the following is most closely related to <u>rapt</u>, as used in the third paragraph?

  a   engrossed

  b   curious

  c   distracted

  d   confused

7. As used in paragraph two, <u>odyssey</u> means

  a   a long journey.

  b   a fast ride.

  c   a short trip.

  d   an intellectual quest.

8. Which profession is most likely to be considered <u>entrepreneurial</u>?

  a   store owner

  b   teacher

  c   football player

  d   doctor

9. Which of the following is not related to <u>infatuated</u>?

  a   love

  b   desire

  c   excess

  d   awareness

10. Which of the following is least related to <u>charisma</u>?

  a   charm

  b   personality

  c   perfection

  d   appeal

SAT Sneak Preview

1. As used in the third paragraph, which of the following is least related to <u>induced</u>?

   (A) taught
   (B) discouraged
   (C) influenced
   (D) persuaded
   (E) suggested

2. As used in paragraph three, <u>rudiments</u> deals with

   (A) vegetables
   (B) ingredients
   (C) basics
   (D) liquids
   (E) balance

3. Which of the following is an antonym for <u>singular</u>?

   (A) popular
   (B) common
   (C) outstanding
   (D) professional
   (E) extraordinary

4. Which of the following is least related to a <u>bastion</u> as used in the fourth paragraph?

   (A) welcoming
   (B) exclusive
   (C) monopoly
   (D) stronghold
   (E) traditional

5. Which of the following is most closely associated with <u>infatuated</u>?

   (A) angry
   (B) disgusted
   (C) upset
   (D) enthusiastic
   (E) obsessed

Answer Key

Lesson 1

1. C
2. D
3. A
4. C
5. B
6. A
7. C
8. B
9. D
10. B
11. C
12. A
13. D
14. C
15. A

SAT

1. D
2. E
3. A
4. B
5. C

Lesson 2

1. B
2. C
3. D
4. A
5. B
6. C
7. B
8. B
9. A
10. D
11. C
12. A
13. D
14. D
15. B

SAT

1. C
2. A
3. D
4. B
5. E

Lesson 3

1. D
2. D
3. A
4. C
5. B
6. C
7. D
8. A
9. B
10. B
11. A
12. A
13. A
14. C
15. B
16. D

SAT

1. A
2. D
3. C
4. B
5. A

Lesson 4

1. D
2. A
3. A
4. B
5. C
6. A
7. C
8. A
9. C
10. A
11. B
12. A
13. D
14. A
15. C

SAT

1. D
2. A
3. E
4. C
5. B

Lesson 5

1. A
2. A
3. C
4. D
5. A
6. D
7. A
8. B
9. B
10. A
11. A
12. D
13. C
14. B
15. A

SAT

1. E
2. B
3. A
4. D
5. C

Lesson 6

1. D
2. B
3. A
4. D
5. A
6. A
7. B
8. A
9. B
10. B
11. B
12. A
13. C
14. C
15. A

SAT

1. D
2. A
3. A
4. E
5. B

Lesson 7

1. A
2. C
3. D
4. A
5. B
6. D
7. A
8. B
9. A
10. B
11. A
12. C
13. A
14. C
15. B

SAT

1. E
2. A
3. D
4. B
5. C

Lesson 8

1. B
2. A
3. A
4. C
5. B
6. C
7. A
8. A
9. D
10. B
11. C
12. C
13. D
14. A
15. B
16. A

SAT

1. A
2. C
3. D
4. B
5. A

Answer Key

Lesson 9

1. B
2. A
3. C
4. D
5. D
6. D
7. B
8. C
9. C
10. B
11. B
12. D
13. A
14. A
15. C

SAT

1. B
2. B
3. E
4. A
5. B

Lesson 10

1. C
2. A
3. A
4. C
5. B
6. B
7. A
8. B
9. C
10. A
11. C
12. D
13. B
14. B
15. D

SAT

1. E
2. A
3. E
4. C
5. A

Midterm Test 1 (Lessons 1–10)

1. B
2. B
3. C
4. A
5. D
6. A
7. D
8. C
9. D
10. A

SAT

1. A
2. A
3. B
4. E
5. C

Midterm Test 2 (Lessons 1–10)

1. B
2. D
3. A
4. D
5. C
6. A
7. B
8. D
9. D
10. A

SAT

1. E
2. A
3. C
4. E
5. B

Lesson 11

1. B
2. A
3. C
4. B
5. A
6. C
7. A
8. A
9. D
10. B
11. D
12. A
13. C
14. D
15. A

SAT

1. C
2. A
3. E
4. D
5. B

Lesson 12

1. A
2. D
3. C
4. A
5. D
6. C
7. A
8. B
9. B
10. B
11. C
12. A
13. C
14. C
15. A

SAT

1. C
2. B
3. C
4. A
5. B

Lesson 13

1. C
2. A
3. A
4. D
5. C
6. A
7. A
8. C
9. A
10. D
11. C
12. A
13. B
14. A
15. A

SAT

1. D
2. A
3. C
4. A
5. C

Lesson 14

1. D
2. B
3. A
4. B
5. D
6. C
7. A
8. B
9. A
10. A
11. D
12. D
13. B
14. A
15. B

SAT

1. A
2. D
3. B
4. E
5. C

Answer Key

Lesson 15

1. C
2. A
3. C
4. B
5. A
6. A
7. D
8. A
9. B
10. D
11. A
12. C
13. C
14. D
15. A

SAT

1. B
2. E
3. A
4. C
5. B

Lesson 16

1. D
2. B
3. A
4. B
5. D
6. A
7. D
8. C
9. B
10. C
11. C
12. D
13. D
14. A
15. A

SAT

1. B
2. A
3. E
4. A
5. C

Lesson 17

1. D
2. A
3. B
4. B
5. A
6. C
7. A
8. D
9. C
10. B
11. C
12. A
13. D
14. A
15. C

SAT

1. E
2. B
3. A
4. D
5. D

Lesson 18

1. D
2. A
3. B
4. C
5. A
6. B
7. D
8. C
9. C
10. C
11. A
12. D
13. D
14. C
15. B

SAT

1. D
2. B
3. E
4. A
5. C

Lesson 19

1. D
2. D
3. A
4. C
5. B
6. A
7. B
8. A
9. D
10. B
11. D
12. C
13. C
14. B
15. C

SAT

1. D
2. A
3. B
4. C
5. E

Lesson 20

1. A
2. C
3. B
4. A
5. C
6. A
7. D
8. C
9. A
10. B
11. C
12. C
13. D
14. C
15. B

SAT

1. A
2. C
3. E
4. B
5. A

Final Test 1
(Lessons 1–20)

1. D
2. A
3. C
4. A
5. C
6. D
7. A
8. B
9. B
10. B

SAT

1. E
2. B
3. A
4. E
5. C

Final Test 2
(Lessons 1–20)

1. C
2. D
3. B
4. B
5. B
6. A
7. C
8. C
9. A
10. C

SAT

1. A
2. E
3. C
4. A
5. D

Answer Key

**Final Test 3
(Lessons 1–20)**

1. C
2. C
3. D
4. A
5. B
6. D
7. D
8. A
9. B
10. A

SAT

1. C
2. A
3. D
4. E
5. B

**Final Test 4
(Lessons 1–20)**

1. C
2. D
3. B
4. D
5. A
6. A
7. D
8. A
9. D
10. C

SAT

1. B
2. C
3. B
4. A
5. E